Easy Machine English Paper Piecing

by Kris Vierra

Fast, Fun Hexie Quilts

Quilter On The Run Press

quilterontherun.com

© K. Vierra

Kris@quilterontherun.com

Easy Machine English Paper Piecing
©2018 by Kris Vierra

Quilter On The Run Press

3500 Daniel Rd
Lincoln, NE 68506-4837
402-484-7858
www.quilterontherun.com

Library of Congress Control Number: 2018942798

Vierra, Kris.

Easy Machine English Paper Piecing/

Kris Vierra.

ISBN 978-1-7322162-0-4

Author's Note

I absolutely hate the words "quilt as desired." I think this phrase should be considered a four letter word. There is nothing worse than getting to the end of a detailed project, pages and pages of instructions on how to construct a top, only to read those dreaded three words "Quilt as Desired." When I first started quilting, I never knew what I desired. Frequently, my finished tops sat for months, or even years, while I tried to figure out what to quilt on them. I vowed, if I ever started writing books or selling patterns, that I would not do this to another person. You will find detailed explanations on how to quilt each project in this book. Please feel free to use them exactly, or as a jumping off point to inspire your own creative ideas. Remember there are no rules. Just enjoy yourself and have fun.

Contents

Introduction......................1

How to use this Book 4

Hexagon Sizing Chart 5

Notes on Fabric 6

Getting Started 7

The Hexies..........................8

Prepping the Hexies 9

Sewing the Hexies............13

Finishing Your Quilt.........15

The Quilts

Flower Power 21

Quilter's Garden 27

Tulips on Parade...............33

Under the Sea 41

Up, Up and Away 51

Flutterby Butterfly............59

Bargello De Hexies 69

Diamonds are a
Girl's Best Friend 81

Star Brite...........................95

Hexagon Jubilee 110

Resources........................ 125

About the Author........... 126

Acknowledgments.......... 127

Introduction

My mom taught me the sewing basics when I was a young girl, and I continued on through 4-H learning how to make and sew garments. It wasn't until my sister had her first baby 20 years ago that I even thought about making a quilt. I started off with that first simple baby quilt and became enthralled with the fascinating and incredibly complex patterns that could be made just by combining fabrics and geometric designs. I became especially intrigued with hexagon quilts. At that time, the only way I knew how to quilt anything, other than a baby quilt, was by hand, and I will freely admit that I am not a good hand quilter. I knew that your stitches were supposed to be nice and even, but mine were always more like Morse code. You know dot, dot, dash, dash, dash. If I'm being honest, I'm not really good at any kind of hand-work. I just don't have the patience, or time, that it takes to become truly proficient. Because of this, I tended to limit myself to small simple square or strip quilt projects, quilts that lent themselves to being tied, but I still dreamed about all of those incredible designs.

Fast forward ten years to when I acquired my Longarm Machine. This opened up all kinds of quilting possibilities for me, but I will concede that my piecing skills were nowhere near as refined as my quilting skills. Starting out as a seamstress, it took me a while to realize that ¼" seams were more than a suggestion. The concepts of sharp points, long straight seams, and smooth curves were great, but how did I achieve them. In addition, there were all these "rules" that I thought I had to follow. Like Y-seams were the only way to connect certain blocks, or the only way to make a hexagon quilt was by hand.

Feeling overwhelmed by these "rules," yet still liking the more complex designs, I started designing my own quilts. These were either: A. whole cloths that didn't require me to piece anything, or B. pictorial quilts that allowed me to do anything I wanted. They didn't have to follow any set "rules," as you could always say that something was "an artistic element" and people wouldn't question anything, but I never forgot those gorgeous, intricately pieced quilts that I first saw when I started with that initial baby quilt. In fact, I had a picture of an antique quilt that I had seen in a book back in 2009, which I could not get out of my head. It was made up of 130, 2" Lemoyne stars that seemed to float across the top of the quilt. The problem was figuring out how to reproduce it. The diamonds needed to make those blocks were only $1\frac{1}{16}$ of an inch with the seam allowance! I tried piecing them by machine without any luck. It's really hard to sew a ½ Y-Seam. Next, I tried having a custom die made to cut them all exactly the same, which helped, but it wasn't enough. I even tried piecing them by hand; I was that desperate. Over the course of the next seven years, I would bring out the fabric and try something different. I just couldn't get this quilt out of my head. Finally, it dawned on me. I was still trying to follow the traditional "rules." Why? Had I not learned anything over the last nine years? Who said there was only one way to make a particular block?

I started thinking about some of the techniques I had used to design my art quilts, and how I might apply these techniques to this star block. It took a few tries, but I finally figured it out. (See the picture to the right of the finished block. Note the thimble for reference, FYI the name of the quilt is Insanity.) Then I got to thinking, I could adapt this same technique to other blocks as well. All those hexagon quilts that I had been so fascinated by were now within my reach! And the best part, not only was the method quick and easy, it was accurate too. This book will take you through all the steps you will need to learn to start making your own gorgeous hexagon quilts. The quilts are in order by difficulty level. Even if you are an accomplished quilter, I recommend starting off with one of the easier projects until you have

mastered the technique. If you are just starting out, don't worry. If you follow the how-to section step-by step, you'll be making perfect hexagon quilts in no time. After that, the sky's the limit!

Insanity

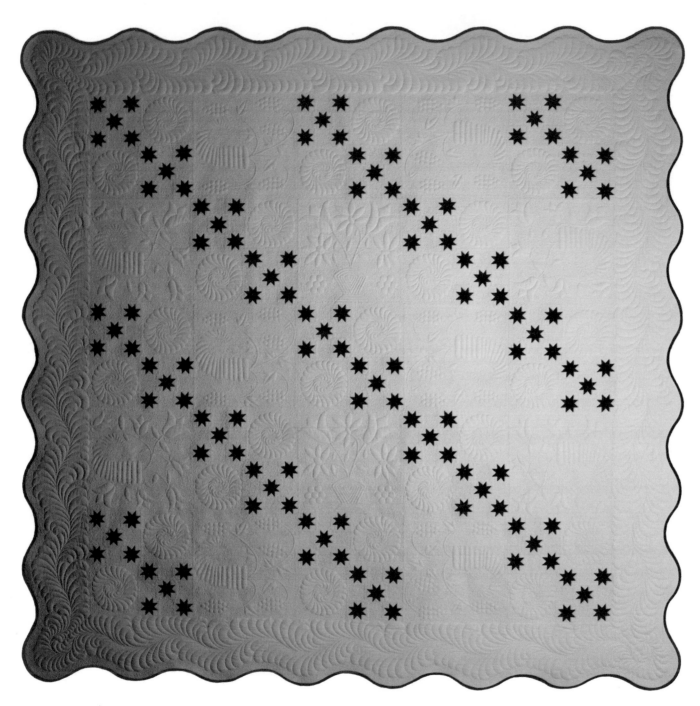

Finished Quilt Size 82" X 82"

Pieced and quilted by the author. ©K. Vierra 2016

How To Use This Book

Flower Power page 21

This book is designed so that the projects get progressively more difficult as you proceed. While you certainly can start with any project, I recommend that you start with *Flower Power*. Even if you only do this one project before moving on to one of the bed sized quilts, I think that you will find that you will have less frustration with the method. Starting with a small quilt will help you to master the technique before you have to manipulate large sections of fabric.

All of the smaller wall hangings, with the exception of *Bargello De Hexagons* are made using ⅝" hexies. *Bargello* and the bed sized quilts are all made with 1" hexies. Hexagons are sized by side length. (See the diagram on the next page for hexagon sizing information.)

Please make sure that you read all of the prep instruction before starting any project. With this method in particular, precision is very important. The more precisely you prepare your hexagons, the better your results. That being said you can still manipulate the hexies fairly easily, if you need to maneuver them to get a better fit.

I highly recommend when learning any new technique that you start by practicing on scrap material. In this case, I would start by making one of the *Standard Flower* sections (instructions on page 14) to familiarize yourself with the process, and to make sure your machine is setup properly, before actually using your project fabric.

Quilters love to share, and I'm no exception. I would love to see any and all projects made from this book. Please feel free to share on my Facebook page (https://www.facebook.com/quilterontherun), or send me an email (kris@quilterontherun.com).

Hexagon Sizing Information

Hexagon Size	Cut Strip Width	# of Pieces a Strip Yields	# of Pieces per Fat Quarter	# of Pieces per 1/4 Yard	# of Pieces per 1/2 yard	# of Pieces per 1 Yard
5/8"	1 3/4"	26	96	96	192	384
3/4"	2"	20	90	90	180	360
1"	2 1/2"	16	57	57	114	228
1 1/4"	3"	13	40	40	80	160
1 1/2"	3 1/2"	11	29	29	58	116

Number of hexagons per strips/yardage is based on 42" wide fabric.

5

I personally recommend pre-washing all of your fabrics. It is very easy to add back in a little extra body or stiffness to the fabric using a spray starch or Best Press ™. It does take a little extra time, but is preferable to having your beautiful quilt marred by a fabric that bled.

Fig. 1

This method does not require you to be concerned with whether you are cutting on the straight or cross grain. Position of the hexies is largely based on personal preference and efficient use of fabric. Depending on the pattern, you may want to *fussy* cut your hexagons to achieve a particular pattern or highlight a section of the fabric. For instance, you could personalize your quilt by positioning the fabric in the center hexagon of each *flower* to focus on something special. (See Fig. 1)

While fabric grain doesn't matter, fabric weave does. Fabrics that fray easily, are very thin, or have an *open* weave, will make handling and working with the hexagons more difficult.

❁ Getting Started ❁

Tools and Supplies

Foundation Paper- *this special paper turns to a soft dissolving fiber when it becomes wet, eliminating the need to remove it. It is thicker than standard wash-away paper allowing you to be able to turn edges with ease. You can order it from www.quilterontherun.com*

Mono-Poly Thread- *Superior®, Madeira® or Sulky® work best*

Machine top-stitch needles 75/11

Elmer's™ Washable School Glue Sticks- *use only this type of glue stick and don't use the disappearing purple sticks.*

Manicure cuticle sticks

Hard Pressing Surface

Freezer paper

♦ Fabric and Paper Scissors

♦ Sewing machine-*with an adjustable zigzag stitch*

♦ Tools for cutting out Hexies- *scissors, Accu-cutter™, Brother Scan and Cut™, rotary cutter*

♦ Wash Cloth-*for cleaning your hands*

❋ The Hexies ❋

Precision is very important to the success of this method, and starts with the foundation hexagons. There are many different ways to make your hexagon *templates*. The easiest is to buy them pre-cut by a laser. This ensures that every hexagon will be exactly the same. You can also cut your own, if you have access to a cutting machine. Brother Scan and Cut™, Cricut™, Accu-cut™ or any equivalent works well. Hexagons can also be traced on the stabilizer using a hexagon template, and then cut out by hand. (*My least favorite method.*)

Note: Accu-cut dies already include seam allowances. If you use one to cut your stabilizer, your hexagons will be ½" bigger than the size marked on the die.

Pre-wash and dry your fabric. After washing, iron fabric with a steam iron. (This would be the time to add starch.) Please note this is the only time you will use steam, after this make sure that you use a DRY IRON only! The stabilizer used in this method is water soluble and will start to dissolve if you use too much steam.

Apply a thin layer of glue to one precut hexagon foundation and affix it to the WRONG SIDE of your fabric. Continue applying hexagons in this manner, making sure to leave ¼" seam allowance on all sides of each of the hexagon. (See Fig. 1)

Fig. 1

Note: Iron your freezer paper to your ironing board for an instant work space. When it gets too much glue on it, just iron another piece on top and continue working.

Note: I like to cut strips of fabric wide enough to accommodate 3-4 hexagons across. These smaller sections are easier to manipulate, when gluing and ironing.

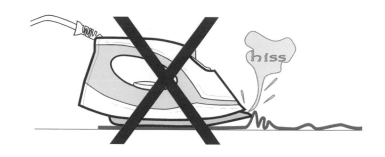

Heat set hexagons with a DRY IRON after gluing. This will help the glue to dry quickly and hold your hexagons more firmly in place.

Note: Place hexagons on point for most efficient use of fabric. (See Fig. 2)

Fig. 2

Cut around stabilizer leaving approximately ¼" seam allowance. This does not need to be exact. If you want them all to be perfect, you can use your rotary cutter and cut each of them out. This will take considerably more time, however, and I personally think it is more fun to sew than to cut. (See Fig. 3)

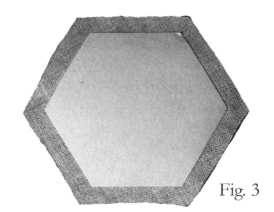

Fig. 3

Note: Exception to rough ¼", if using the hexagon facing method to finish a quilt, you will need to make sure that you have an exact ¼" seam allowance. (See Finishing Your Quilt page 15)

pply a thin layer of Elmer's School
Glue™ to two opposing sides of
the hexagon. Fold seam allowance towards
stabilizer. If you are having difficulty turning
the edges, try using the flat side of the
manicure stick. Repeat on opposite sides until
all sides of the hexagon have been turned
towards the stabilizer. (Figs. 1-3)

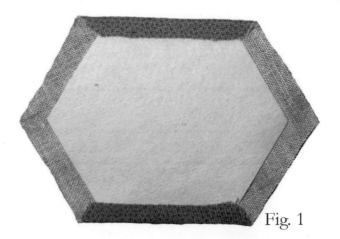

Fig. 1

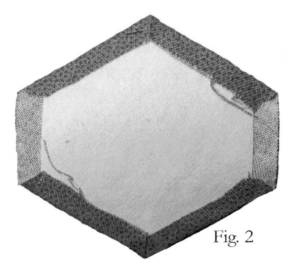

Fig. 2

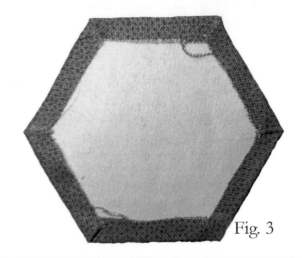

Fig. 3

I recommend using a hexagon template on
all of your hexagons in the beginning, to
check for accuracy. The more hexagons you
make, the better, and faster, you will get at
folding the fabric on to the foundation paper.
As you become more proficient, you may only
need to spot check one out of every 10-15
hexagons. (See Fig. 4)

**Note: If using a template with
seam allowance shown, use
the finished hexagon size for
spot checking.**

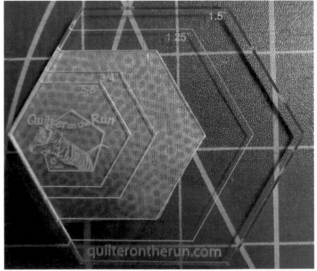

Fig. 4

Be gentle when turning hexie sides. The more precisely you turn the fabric onto the foundation hexagon, the better the final fit of the top. Watch out for overturning the sides. This results when you have too much glue which softens the paper, or just being a little to rough. When this happens, both the fabric and the foundation paper get turned under, creating a *dip* in the side. (See Fig. 5)

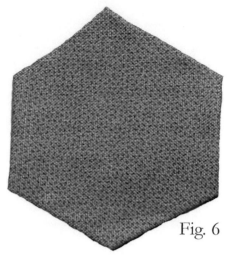

Fig. 6

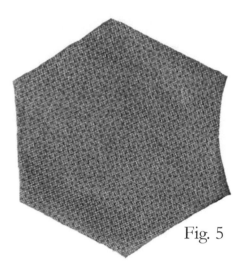

Fig. 5

Both underturning and overturning will cause problems during the assembly process. You might not notice it as much when joining together individual hexies, but as you continue to assemble the quilt, it will become more pronounced. Just like in standard piecing when you don't have an accurate $\frac{1}{4}$" seam allowance.

The reverse occurs when you don't turn the fabric over onto the foundation paper far enough. This causes the hexagons to have an irregular shape, and will affect how well the hexagons fit together in the finished top. (See Fig. 6)

Sewing The Hexies

Set your sewing machine to a *zig-zag* stitch. I recommend a very short stitch length, and a narrow width. When you are just starting out, you may want to increase your stitch width, but don't change your stitch length. You will also need to decrease your top tension on your sewing machine when you are using mono-poly thread. (The settings shown in Fig. 1 are for my Bernina. You will need to adjust accordingly for your machine.)

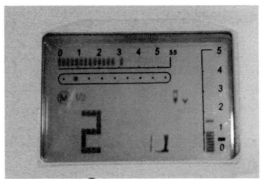
Fig. 1

Take two hexies and butt the edges closely together. Make sure that they are closely touching, but not overlapping. Align the top and bottom edges making sure that they are even. (See Fig 2)

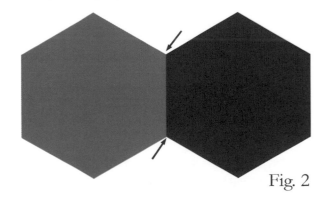
Fig. 2

Secure your starting stitch and continue stitching using your narrow *zig-zag* stitch. Make sure that the needle goes from one hexie to the other. This will ensure that your hexies are securely fastened to each other. (See Fig 3)

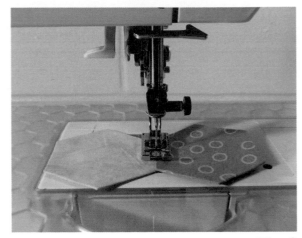
Fig. 3

Each quilt pattern shows the most efficient hexagon groupings. Following the pattern order, sew your next hexagon in place. (See Fig. 4)

Fig. 4

The central unit of most hexagon quilts is the *standard flower* section. Sew hexagons in the order shown in Fig. 5. The most efficient way to quilt a *standard flower* section is to stitch down one side, backtrack, and then stitch up the opposite side. (See stitching diagram below.) This eliminates the need to constantly stop and start. Continue in this fashion until entire *flower* section is assembled.

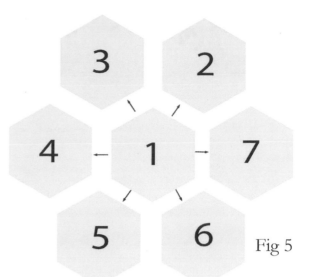

Fig 5

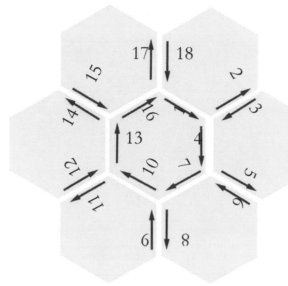

Stitching Diagram

Sew the required number of each hexagon *grouping* together, as per the pattern directions. After all *groupings* have been completed, join sections together as directed in the pattern. If needed, you can ease sections together slightly. Don't worry if sections bow slightly. They will flatten out when quilted or washed.

For quilts that have the hexagons *set* on top of a background fabric, apply a thin layer of glue to the entire hexagon figure and center onto the background fabric. Use the placement diagram as a reference. Heat set and then sew along the edge using the same *zig-zag* stitch used to assemble the hexies. Make sure that the needle catches the hexie with one stitch and the background fabric with the next stitch.

Note: be careful about placing light hexagons on a dark background. The stabilizer keeps the dark fabric from initially shadowing through the lighter fabric, but remember it will be washed away.

The quilts in this book are finished in one of two ways: traditional binding, or facing. All of the wall hangings with the exception of *Up, Up and Away* are bound. *Up, Up and Away* is faced. Facing is an alternative method for finishing the raw edges of the quilt sandwich, without needing to apply a traditional binding.

As everyone's sewing machine is just slightly different, I give general sizes for borders and then you can adjust as necessary using the method described below. If you wish to miter the corners of your borders, allow for an additional 10"-12" of fabric length per border.

Hexagon quilts can be completed in one of three ways: cutting the hexies to create an even edge to bind, appliquéing the hexies to a border and then binding as normal, or facing the hexagons. The first method is used on *Diamonds Are A Girl's Best Friend* and *Bargello De Hexies*. The appliqué method is used on *Star Brite*, and *Hexagon Jubilee* is faced. Appliquéing and facing the hexies allows you to keep the full hexagonal form and retain its traditional charm. (All of the wall hangings have a standard binding except for *Up, Up and Away*, which is faced.

To figure out the width of your borders, measure your quilt at the top, the bottom, and in the middle. Add these numbers together and divide by three. This will give you the correct width. Repeat, measuring the left and right sides from top to bottom and middle of your quilt to determine the border length

Cutting The Hexies

After your top is entirely pieced, but not yet quilted, lay it out on a flat surface. I find that a large table works well. With your cutting mat underneath the quilt, lay a long acrylic ruler along the edge of the top. Align the ruler with the bottom of the "V" made by the hexies. (See Fig. 1)

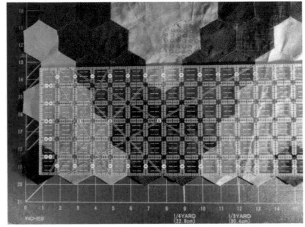

Fig. 1

Using your rotary cutter, cut off all the points. (See Fig. 2)

Fig. 2

15

Continue cutting, using the same method, until you have reached the corner. When you get to the next side, align your ruler with the flat side of the inner hexies. (See Fig. 3)

Fig. 3

Continue cutting until you have gone all the way around the quilt. (See Fig. 4) You can now apply your borders and quilt your quilt and then apply a traditional binding. I recommend cutting your binding strips 2" wide, if you are using a double fold binding, and $1\frac{1}{4}$" wide, if you are using a single fold.

Fig. 4

Appliquéing the Hexies

For this method, you will need to cut your border strips to different widths. You will need (2) 2" wide by roughly 8" longer than the length of the quilt, and (2) $2\frac{1}{4}$" wide by roughly 8" longer than the width of the quilt. Using a long acrylic ruler, draw a line on the back of the quilt $\frac{1}{4}$" below the edge of the inner hexies. (See Fig 1 & 2)Repeat on the opposite side.

Fig. 1

Fig. 2

Turn quilt and mark a line $\frac{1}{2}$" below the inner "V" points of the hexagons. (See Fig. 3 on the following page)

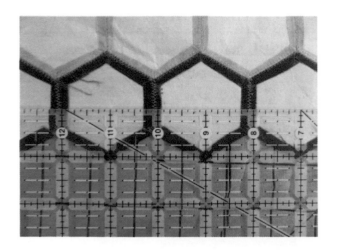

Fig. 3

Apply a thin layer of glue to the wrong side of the top between the line marked previously and the top of the hexies. Carefully lay one of the border strips on top of the glued section lining up the bottom edge of the strip with the marked line. (The 2" strips go on the sides with the pointed hexies and the $2\frac{1}{4}$" strips on the sides with the flat hexies.) Stop gluing 4-5 hexies from the end (See Figs. 4 & 5)

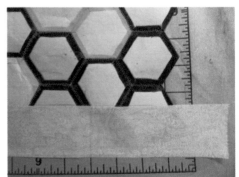

Fig. 4

Fig. 5

Apply strips to all four sides. Using a narrow *zig-zag* stitch, stitch hexies to border fabric. Make sure to start and stop stitching 4-5 hexies from the end of the top. Align needle so that one side of the *zig-zag* runs right along the edge of the hexies. (See Fig. 6)

Fig. 6

Fold one border side up at a 45 degree angle. (See Fig. 7) Check alignment using an acrylic ruler. (See Fig. 8)

Fig. 7

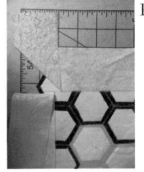

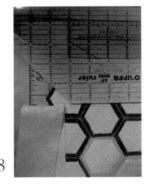

Fig. 8

Run a thin bead of glue along the folded edge. (See Fig. 9 on the following page) Carefully lay other border on top of glued strip and heat set with a dry iron. Bottom edges should not be even. (See Fig. 10 on the following page)

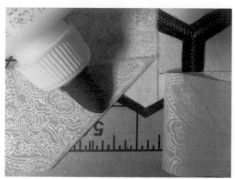

Fig. 9

Fig. 10

Open up the fold. Making sure that the hexies are out of the way, sew along the crease. (See Fig. 11)

Fig. 11

Open and press seam. (See Fig 12) Trim to roughly ¼"; press again. (See Fig. 13)

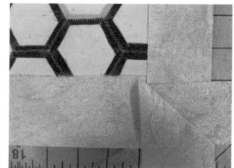

Fig. 12

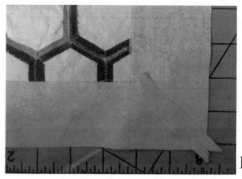

Fig. 13

Apply a thin layer of glue to the wrong side of the top between the previously marked line and the top of the remaining hexies. Stitch border to the hexies left unstitched initially. (Fig. 14)

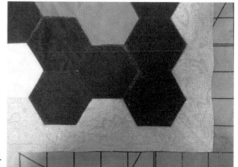

Fig. 14

Facing The Hexies

With this method, the hexies around the edge of the quilt will be treated a little differently than usual. These hexies will need to be cut to an exact ¼" using a rotary cutter. Following the directions in the quilt assembly section, the outer edges will not be turned under. Make sure to not prep these hexies until instructed.

Quilt top as per directions (or your choosing). This method is easiest if you stop quilting approximately ¼"- ½" from the edges. After quilting, carefully trim batting and backing even with hexie edges. (See Fig. 1 on the following page.)

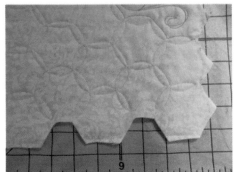

Fig. 1

Turn quilt so that backing is facing up and carefully trim away slightly more than ¼" of the backing and batting only, being careful not to trim the hexies. (See Fig. 2)

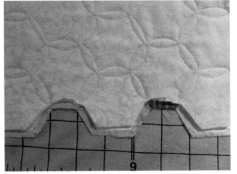

Fig. 2

Cut facing as per directions in quilt pattern section. Fold over one long edge ½" and press. (See Fig. 3)

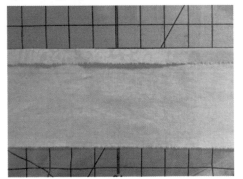

Fig. 3

Apply a thin layer of glue along the edge of the hexies as per Fig. 4. Carefully lay one prepared facing strip along the glued hexies; heat seat with a dry iron. (See Fig. 5) Edges of facing strip should extend slightly past the edges of the quilt.

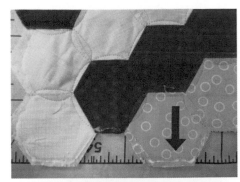

Fig. 4

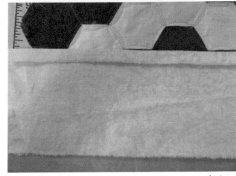

Fig. 5

With backing side up, carefully align ¼" foot with th edge of the hexies. (See Fig. 6) Leaving the needle down, pivot and sew up the next side. (See Fig. 7) Continue until you have completely sewn one entire facing strip. Repeat on the opposite side of the quilt.

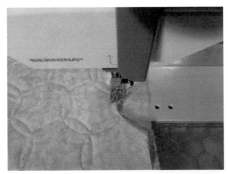

Fig. 6

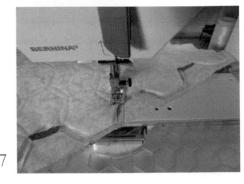

Fig. 7

Carefully trim away facing strip so that it is even with the hexies. Trim corners and clip to seam at pivot points, taking care not to clip stitching. (See Fig. 8 & 9)

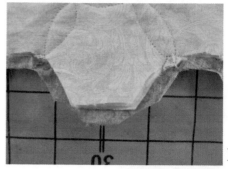

Fig. 8

Fig. 9

Using one of the remaining precut facing strips, fold under ½" and press. Apply a thin line of glue to the tops of side hexies the same as you did on the top and bottom. Lay facing strip carefully on top of the glue. Heat set with a dry iron. Facing strip should be shorter than the length of the quilt by approximately 1" on each side. (See Fig. 10)

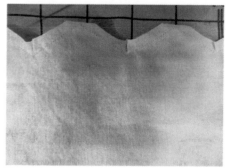

Fig. 10

Using the method described previously sew facing to quilt; trim, and clip to seams. (See Fig. 11) Repeat on opposite side.

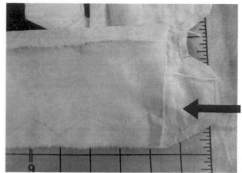

Fig. 11

Turn facing to back of quilt. Using the orange stick gently push out the points and corners of the hexies. Using a blind stitch sew facing to back of quilt. (See Fig 12)

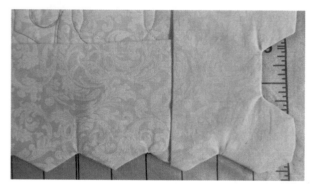

Fig. 12

After you have applied your choice of binding method, you can then wash your quilt. I recommend washing quilts on delicate and laying flat or tumbling dry on low. The longer you soak your quilt the more the stabilizer will dissolve, and the softer your quilt will become.

Flower Power

Finished Quilt Size 25" X 31"

Get your groove on with this sixties inspired flower power wall hanging that's just the right size to brighten any room.

Materials

Yardage is based on 42" wide fabric

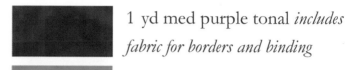 1 yd med purple tonal *includes fabric for borders and binding*

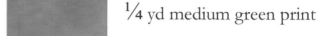 ¼ yd medium green print

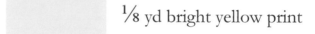 ⅛ yd bright yellow print

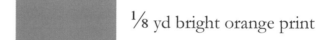 ⅛ yd bright orange print

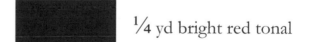 ¼ yd bright red tonal

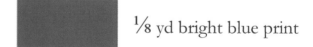 ⅛ yd bright blue print

 1 yd light blue

1 yard of your choice of coordinating fabric for backing.

Hexie Requirements (⅝")

 6 yellow hexagons

 6 blue hexagons

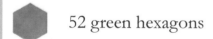 52 green hexagons

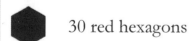 30 red hexagons

 13 purple hexagons

 18 orange hexagons

Total number of hexagon foundations needed for this project: 125.

Assembling the Quilt

Prepare the required number of each color hexagons, as per the instructions in the *Prepping The Hexies* section. (Page 9)

From light blue fabric cut:

(1) 25½" X 31½"

From med/dark purple tonal cut:

(2) 1½" X 29½"

(2) 1½" X 25½"

1. Sew together (1) yellow and (1) purple hexagon. Continue around the center hexagons to create the center *standard flower,* as per instructions in Sewing the Hexagons on page 14. (See Fig. 1)

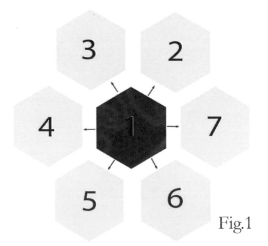

Fig.1

2. Sew the next row onto the flower alternating red and blue hexagons. Make sure that the blue hexagons are sewn into the "V's" and the red hexagons are sewn on to the flat sides of the yellow hexagons. (See Fig. 2)

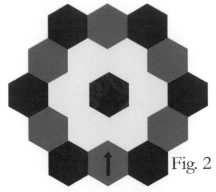

Fig. 2

3. Sew a third row of red hexagons on to this unit. (See Fig. 3)

Fig. 3

4. Sew together two orange hexagons to make a double orange unit. Next make a double unit using one purple and one red hexagon; repeat for a total of (6) double orange and (6) double red/purple units.

5. Sew a third orange hexagon on to the (2) orange hexagon unit; repeat for a total of (6) units. (See Fig. 4)

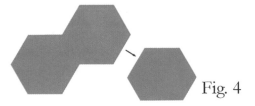

Fig. 4

6. Sew an additional purple hexagon on to the red and purple hexagon unit; repeat for a total of (6) units. (See Fig. 5 on the following page)

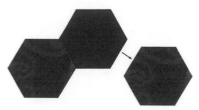

Fig. 5

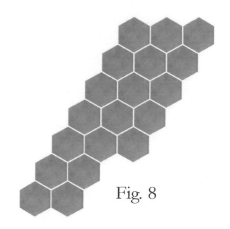

Fig. 8

7. Connect (1) orange hexagon unit to (1)red and purple unit. (See Fig. 6)

Fig. 6

8. Attach orange, red, and purple units to center flower section. (See Fig. 7)

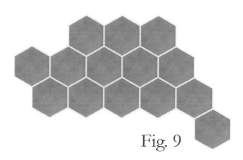

Fig. 9

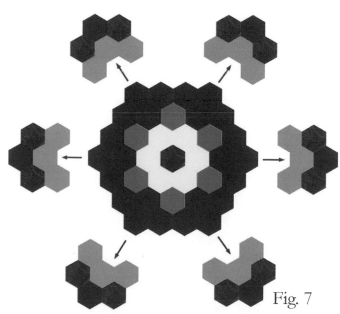

Fig. 7

9. Sew together (2) green hexagons; repeat for a total of four units. Sew together (3) green hexagons; repeat until you have (7) units. Sew together (4) green hexagons. Sew these units together to form leaves (See Fig. 8 and Fig. 9)

10. Using placement diagram on page 25, sew together remaining green hexagons to form flower stem. Join flower and leaves to stem.

11. Apply a thin layer of glue to wrong side of finished flower, and center on blue background fabric using placement diagram on page 25 as a guide.

12. Apply purple borders to sides and top. Press seams towards away from center. Quilt as per quilting diagram on page 26. Background was quilted using a meandering filigree type design. Leaves were outlined and details were added to form spines. Swirls were quilted onto the flower petals.

Placement Diagram

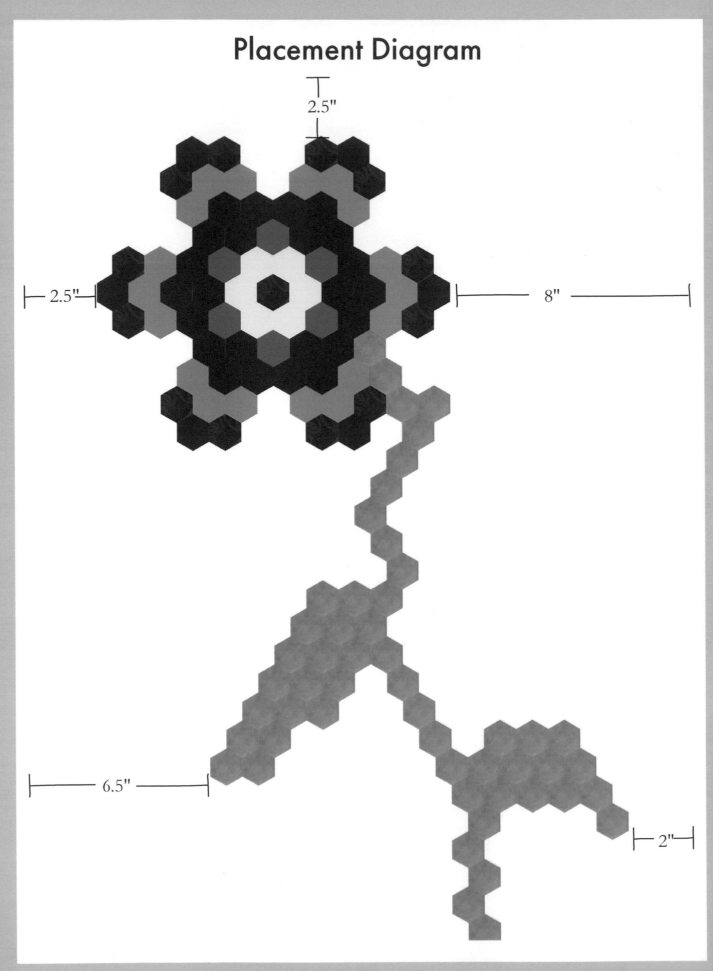

Quilting Diagram

A Quilter's Garden

Finish Quilt Size 48" X 66"

Lap quilts provide a cozy feeling no matter what the weather. Snuggle up under this cute hexie quilt with twinkling star flowers climbing this easy vine.

Materials

Yardage is based on 42" wide fabric

 2 yds med/dark purple print *(includes border and binding)*

 1¾ yds medium blue print *(includes inner border)*

 1⅝ yd light blue fabric

 ¼ yd med/dark red print

 ⅛ yd medium yellow print

 ⅜ yd medium green tonal

3 yds of your choice of coordinating fabric for backing. (Backing will be seamed.)

Hexie Requirements (⅝")

 140 green hexagons

 94 purple hexagons

 94 blue hexagons

 94 red hexagons

 21 yellow hexagons

Total number of hexagon foundations needed for this project: 443

Assembling the Quilt

Prepare the required number of each color hexagons, as per the instructions in the *Prepping the Hexies* section. (Page 9)

***

From blue fabric cut:
(2) 2½" X 54½"
(2) 2½" X 40½"
From purple fabric cut:
(2) 4½" X 58½"
(2) 4½" X 48½"
From light blue background cut:
(1) 36½" X 54½"

***

1. Join together (2) blue hexagons; repeat until you have (12) units. Add a third blue hexagon to half of the units. Repeat for each of the red and purple *hexagon flowers*. (See Fig. 1)

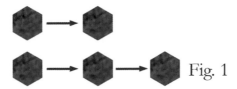

Fig. 1

2. Using (1) additional blue hexagon, join your (3) hexagon unit to a your (2) hexagon unit, placing one additional hexagon on top, as per Fig. 2. For each color flower: red, blue and purple, make (6) units.

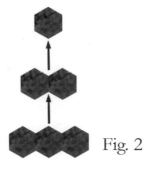

Fig. 2

3. Begin by sewing together (2) yellow hexagons. Referring to Fig. 3, continue to add hexagons in numerical order until center yellow unit is completed.

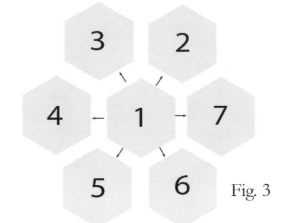

Fig. 3

4. Continue, referring to Fig. 4, to sew three concentric rows of blue hexagons around this yellow center. Repeat process to make red and purple *flower* centers.

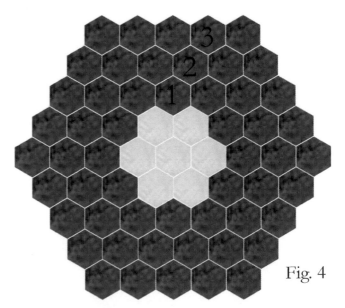

Fig. 4

5. Attach units made in steps 1 and 2 to the flower center made in step 4. (See Fig. 5 on the following page.)

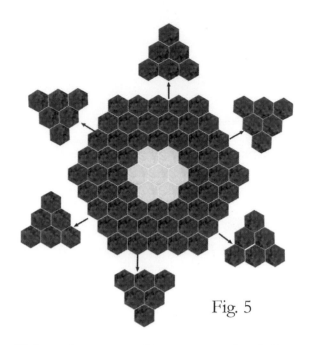

Fig. 5

6. Using placement diagram on the following page as a reference, join together green hexagons to form vines. I find it's easiest to string piece a bunch of hexies into units of two, and then start to join those double units together to make larger units. Do not join all of the hexagons into double units as you will need some odd numbered ones. Continue joining green hexagons until vine is completed. Attach vine to flowers.

7. Apply a thin layer of glue to the back of the finished unit. Using placement guide on page 31 as a reference, affix hexagons to the $36\frac{1}{2}$" X $54\frac{1}{2}$" piece of light blue back ground fabric. Heat fix with dry iron, and sew together using *zig-zag* stitch.

8. If needed, adjust the inner blue side borders using the method to find correct border size listed in the *Finishing Your Quilt* pg 15.

9. Apply borders to sides of quilt using a $\frac{1}{4}$" seam allowance. Press all seams out and away from center. Repeat with inner top/bottom blue border strips, adjusting as needed to fit quilt. Using same $\frac{1}{4}$" seam allowance apply to top and bottom of quilt. Allow extra length, if mitering the corners.

10. Repeat using outer purple side and top/bottom borders.

11. Refer to quilting diagram on page 32 for quilting ideas. Quilt was quilted using freehand feathers around the outer border, and loops in the inner border. A simple swirl sets off the *flower vines*, and is echoed inside the main hexagon *flowers*. A generic meander was used to quilt the background. Optional: I recommend outline quilting around the outer edge of the hexagons for more definition.

Placement Diagram

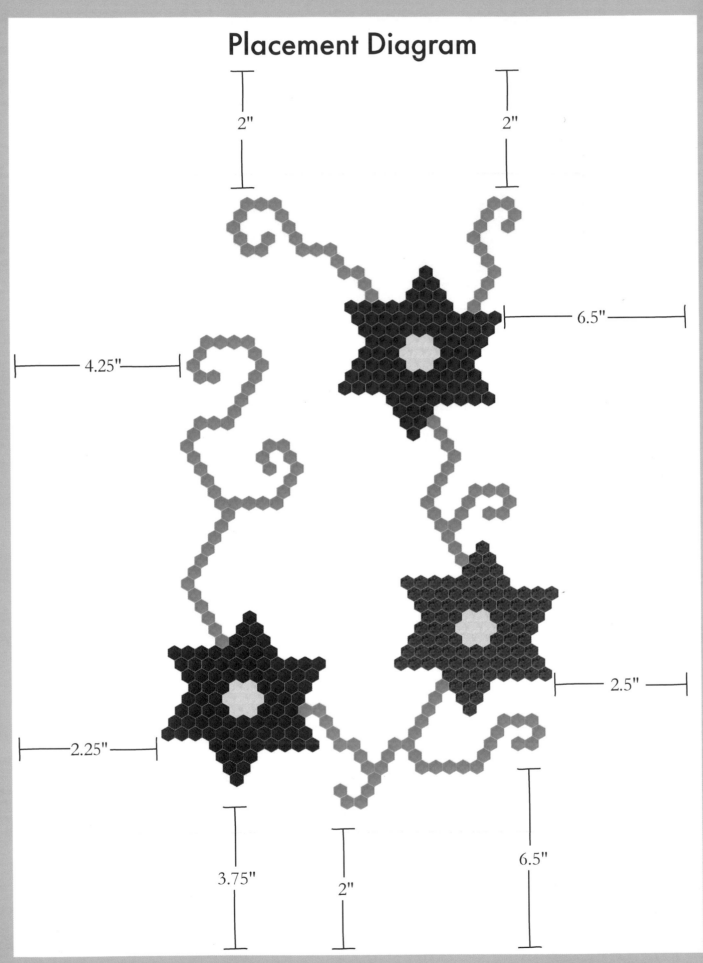

Quilting Diagram

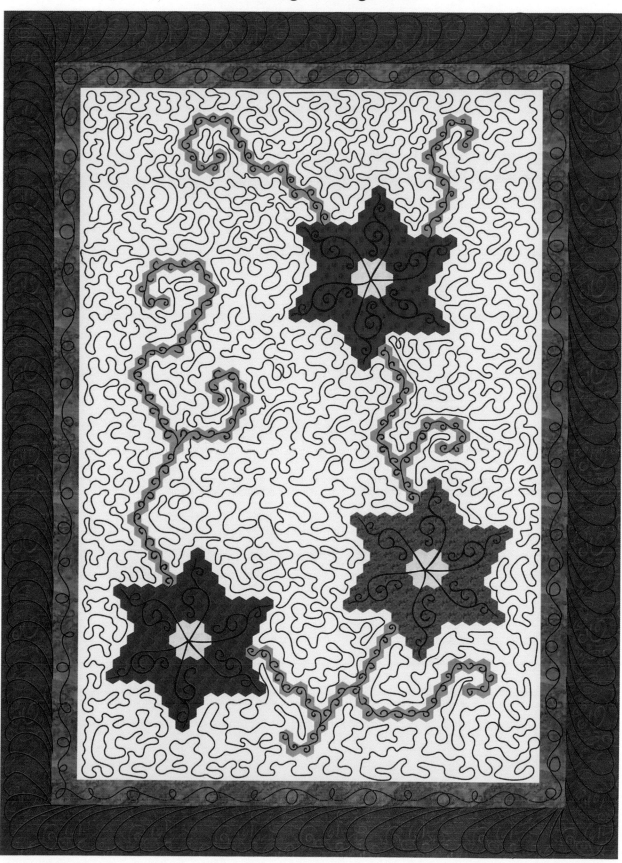

Tulips on Parade

Finished Quilt Size 45"X65"

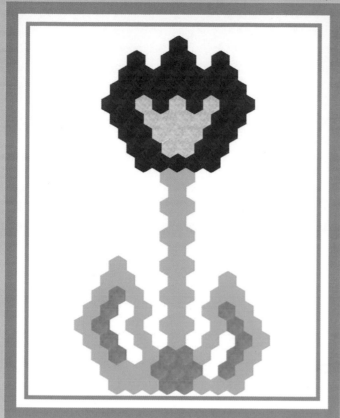

You don't have to wait for spring to enjoy the tulips. This jubilee of hexie flowers will let you plant a truly colorful garden any time of year.

Materials

Yardage is based on 42" wide fabric

Fat quarter med. pink print

2 yds red tonal *includes borders and binding*

Fat quarter light purple print

¼ yd purple tonal

Fat quarter med. orange print

⅛ yd dark orange tonal

¼ yd light/med green print

⅜ yd med/dark green print

1⅓ yds light blue fabric

1½ yds of your choice of coordinating fabric for backing.

Hexie Requirements (⅝")

12 medium pink hexagons

43 red hexagons

43 purple hexagons

12 light purple hexagons

43 medium orange hexagons

12 dark orange hexagons

80 light/medium green hexagons

162 medium/dark green hexagons

Total number of hexagon foundations needed for this project: 407.

Assembling the Quilt

Prepare the required number of each color hexagons, as per the instructions in the *Prepping the Hexies* section. (Page 9)

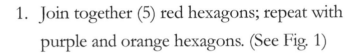

From light blue fabric cut:
(1) 31½" X 44½"
From purple tonal cut
(2) 2½" X 31½"
(2) 2½" X 48½"

1. Join together (5) red hexagons; repeat with purple and orange hexagons. (See Fig. 1)

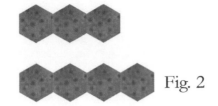

Fig. 2

5. Join one double red hexagon unit to either side of the (2), (3) and (4) pink chains previously made; repeat with the light purple and dark orange units, using the previously made purple and orange units respectively. (See Fig. 3)

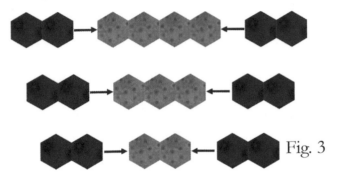

Fig. 3

1. Join together (5) red hexagons; repeat with purple and orange hexagons. (See Fig. 1)

Fig. 1

2. Join (2) red hexies, repeat for a total of (16) double hexie units; repeat process with purple and orange hexagons.

3. Join together (2) pink; repeat until you have (4) double pink units. Repeat this process using the light purple and dark orange hexagons.

4. Using (3) of the pink double hexie units made in Step 2, add one additional pink hexagon to one of the double units to make a (3) hexie chain, and join the other (2) of them together to make a chain of (4) hexagons; repeat with the light purple and dark orange units. (See Fig. 2)

6. Join a pink hexagon to a red hexagon, repeat for a total of (2) units. Repeat process using light purple and dark orange hexagons

7. Join the pink/red unit to the other pink/ red unit and add one additional pink unit to the end. This will make a (5) hexagon chain. Repeat using light purple/purple, dark orange/orange units. (See Fig. 4)

Fig. 4

8. Using the double hexagon units from step 2, join one double red unit to each side of the (5) hexagon chain made in the previous step. Repeat using purple and orange units. (See Fig. 5)

Fig. 5

9. Using the red double hexagons units from step 2, join (4) double hexagons together to make one chain (8) hexagons long.

10. Join (3) additional red double hexies together to make a chain (6) hexies long. Add one red hexagon to the end of this chain for a total of (7) hexies; repeat using purple and orange units.

11. Using the red double hexie units from step 2, add a single hexagon to the top of one of the double red units to form a pyramid shape; repeat for a total of (3) units. Repeat this using the purple and orange double units. (See Fig. 6)

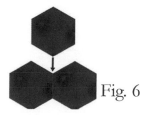

Fig. 6

12. Add an additional red hexie to (1) of the remaining red double hexagon units to form a (3) hexie chain.

13. Join one of the *pyramids* to the (3) hexagon chain made in step 12 Repeat using purple and orange hexagons. (See Fig. 7)

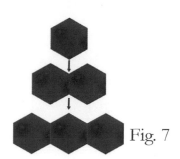

Fig. 7

14. Using Fig. 8 as a guide sew the previously made rows together to create the tulips.

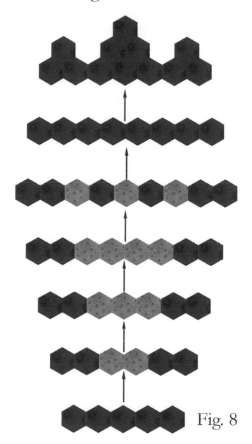

Fig. 8

15. Join together (2) dark green hexagons; repeat for a total of (22) double hexie units. Add one dark green hexagon to the top of one of these double units; repeat for a total of (20) units. (See Fig. 9)

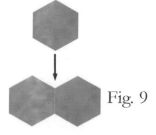

Fig. 9

16. Join (10) of the units made in the previous step together to form the stem. Add the remaining double dark green hexagon unit to the bottom of this chain; repeat to form both dark green stems. (See Fig 10)

17. Using the same technique create and join together (6) light green units. (See Fig. 11)

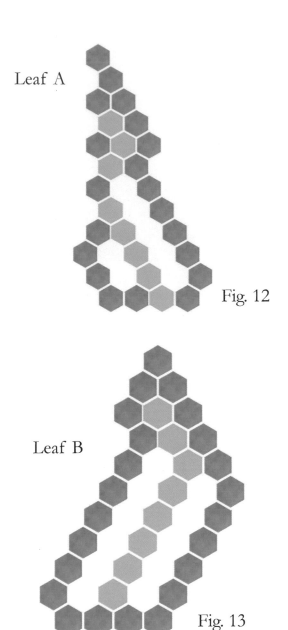

Leaf A

Fig. 12

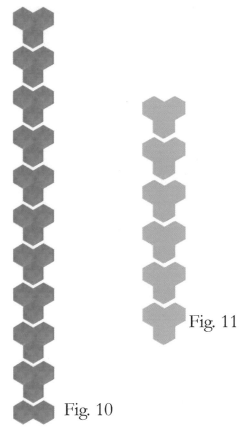

Fig. 11

Fig. 10

Leaf B

Fig. 13

18. Using Figures 12-17 on the following pages as reference, join together remaining dark and light green hexagons to form the leaves. Figures go in order from left to right for leaf placement.

19. Join leaves to each side of previously made stems and sew tulip to tops of stems using placement guide on page 39 as a reference.

Leaf C

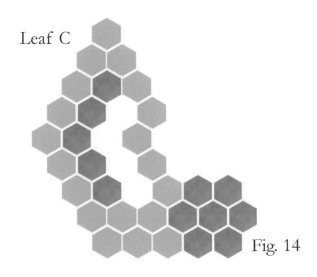

Fig. 14

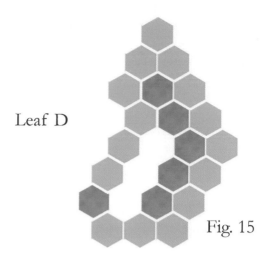

Leaf D

Fig. 15

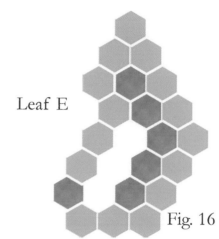

Leaf E

Fig. 16

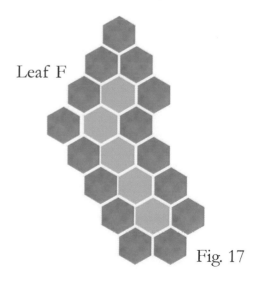

Leaf F

Fig. 17

20. Connect the (3) tulips to each other. Apply a thin layer of glue to the back of the tulips and center them on the light blue fabric. Heat set with a dry iron, and *zigzag* around the outside edge to secure them to the background fabric. (If you are having trouble maneuvering the larger unit, you can glue each tulip on individually. Just remember to *zigzag* the units together once they are on the background fabric. This avoids having any loose edges.)

21. Apply side borders using a ¼" seam allowance; repeat with top and bottom borders. Press seams towards borders.

22. Quilt was quilted using assorted variegated thread. Swirls and ribbons were quilted in the stems and leaves. More swirls were quilted onto each tulip. I meandered in the background using light blue thread. The border was quilted using half of a feathered vine with pink variegated thread. See quilting diagram on page 40, as a reference.

Placement Diagram

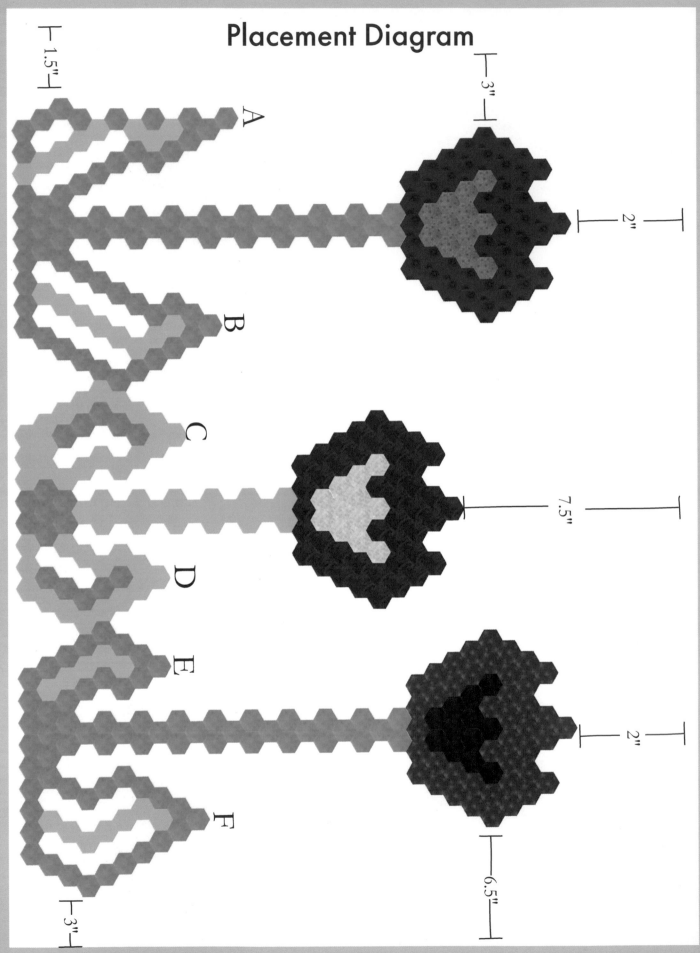

39

Quilting Diagram

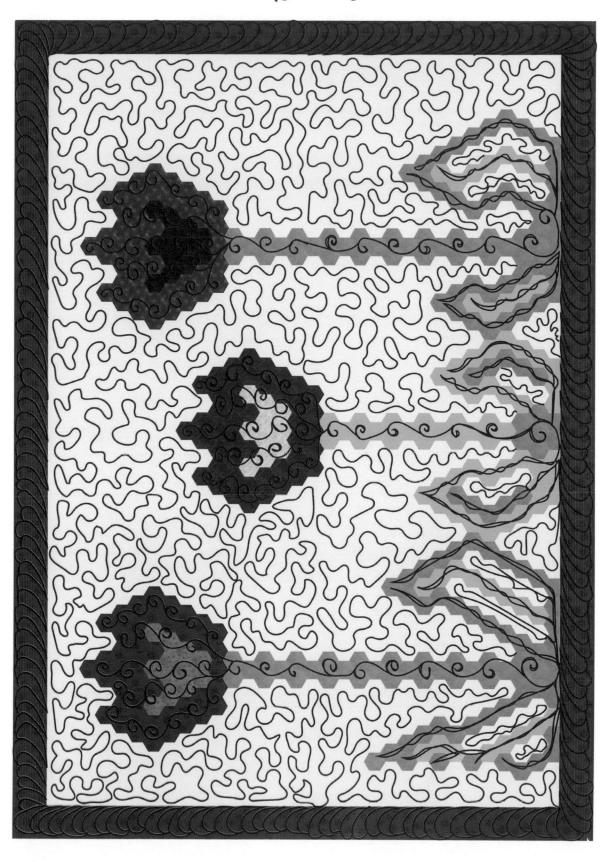

Under the Sea

Finished Tote Size 21"X 16.5"

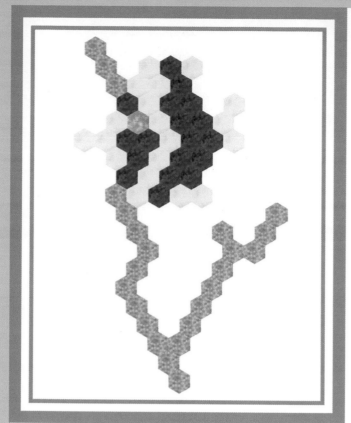

A quilter can never have too many totes. These hexie fish are a swimmingly perfect way to store and carry all your quilting supplies.

Materials

Yardage is based on 42" wide fabric

 3 yds light/med blue tonal batik *background and lining for bag*

 ¼ yd medium green print

 ⅛ yd bright yellow print

 ¼ yd bright pink print

 ⅛ yd med/dark red solid

 ⅛ yd dark blue tonal

 Small scrap dark purple/red for large fish's eye

1½ yards medium blue batik for background, lining, pocket and straps. ¾ yard 48" wide muslin for backing. (This will be covered by the lining, and will not be visible.

Hexie Requirements (⅝")

 74 med green hexagons

 48 bright yellow hexagons

 41 dark blue hexagons

 107 bright pink hexagons

 102 med/dark red hexagons

 1 dark purple/red hexagons

Total number of hexagon foundations needed for this project: 373.

Assembling the Quilt

Prepare the required number of each color hexagons, as per the instructions in the *Prepping the Hexies* section. (Page 9)

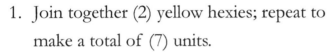

From medium blue batik cut:

(2) 42" X 17½"

(2) 17½" X 5"

(2) 4" X 32"

(1) 8½" X 15"

1. Join together (2) yellow hexies; repeat to make a total of (7) units.

2. Join together (2) blue hexies; repeat for a total of (8) units.

3. Join a third yellow hexie to one of the yellow units made in step 1; repeat for a total of (2) units. (See Fig. 1)

Fig. 1

4. To one of the units made in step 3 add a fourth yellow hexie. (See Fig. 2)

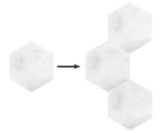

Fig. 2

5. Join together (1) blue hexie and (1) pink hexie. Join this unit and (2) of the double blue hexie units together. (See Fig. 3)

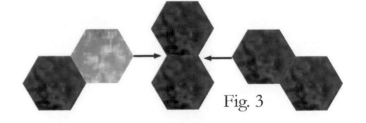

Fig. 3

6. Join together (2) of the double yellow units to make one (4) hexie chain. Add (2) additional double units to the ends of this (4) hexie chain. (See Fig. 4)

Fig. 4

7. Stagger sew (6) of the double blue hexie units together. Add (1) yellow hexie to the top of this group. (See Fig. 5)

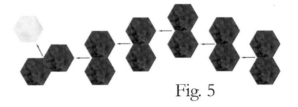

Fig. 5

8. Join together the units made in steps 1-8. (See Fig. 6)

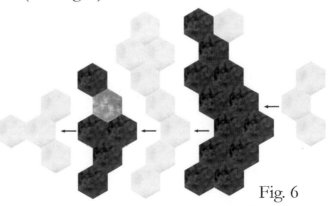

Fig. 6

9. Join (1) yellow hexie to (1) blue hexie. Attach this unit to one of the previously assembled (2) yellow units. (See Fig. 7)

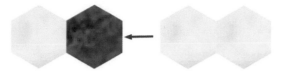

Fig. 7

10. Add the unit made in step 9 to the hexies assembled in step 8. (See Fig. 8)

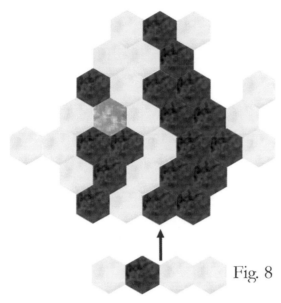

Fig. 8

11. Repeat steps 1-10 to make the second blue and yellow fish.

Big Fish Assembly

1. Combine (7) bright pink hexies to form one *standard flower* unit, as per the instructions in Sewing the Hexagons on page 14; repeat for a total of 4 units. (See Fig. 9)

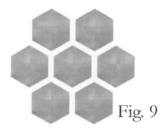

Fig. 9

2. Join together (2) red hexies; repeat (40) times. Join (1) additional red hexie to (16) of the double units. (See Fig. 10)

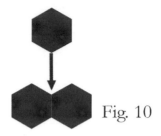

Fig. 10

3. Combine two (2) hexie and two (3) hexie units to form Unit 1. (See Fig. 11)

4. Join together (2) bright pink hexies; repeat (33) times. Add an additional pink hexie to (6) of these units. Replicating the red units in pink (See Fig. 10)

5. Sew together (1) bright pink and (1) dark purple hexie.

6. Combine the pink/purple unit, (1) *standard flower* unit, (2) double pink units, one (3) pink unit, and one additional pink hexie to form Unit 2. (See Fig. 12)

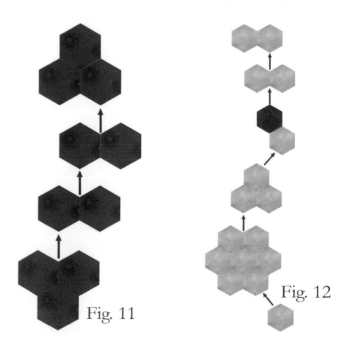

Fig. 11

Fig. 12

7. Combine (4) double red units and (4) red (3) hexie units together to make Unit 3. (See Fig. 13)

8. Using (2) pink *standard flower* units, (6) double pink units, and one additional pink hexie, sew together to form Unit 4. (See Fig. 14)

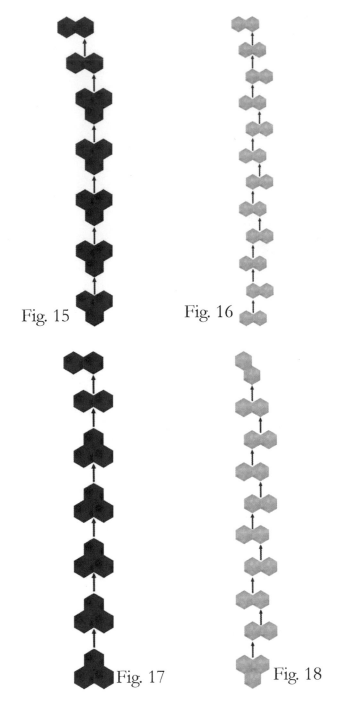

Fig. 15

Fig. 16

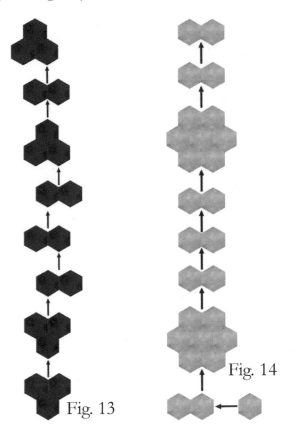

Fig. 13

Fig. 14

Fig. 17

Fig. 18

9. Combine (5) red three hexie units with (2) red double hexie units to form Unit 5. (See Fig 15)

10. Sew together (12) double pink hexie units to form Unit 6. (See Fig. 16)

11. Combine (5) red three hexie units and (2) double red hexie units to form Unit 7. (See Fig. 17)

12. Sew together (1) pink three hexie unit and (9) pink double hexie units to form Unit 8. (See Fig. 18)

13. Combine (2) red double hexie units and one additional red hexie to form Unit 9. (See Fig. 19 opposite page)

14. Using remaining triple pink hexie units and (1) additional pink hexie, sew together to form Unit 10. (See Fig. 20, opp. pg)

15. Sew together the remaining pink *standard flower* unit and Units 1-10 to form body of large fish. (See Fig. 21 opposite pg)

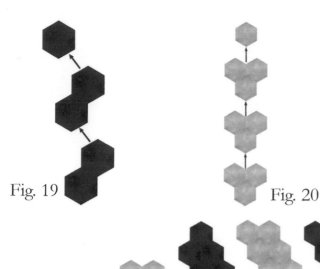

Fig. 19

Fig. 20

19. Join (3) red double hexie units to make a chain of (6) hexies; repeat to make (2) chains (6) hexies long.

20. Join red/yellow units together alternating red/yellow units for a total of (6) hexies.

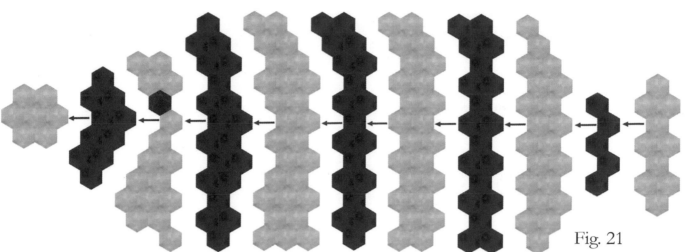

Fig. 21

16. Join together (5) red double hexie units to form a chain of (10).

17. Sew together (2) bright yellow hexies; repeat (3) times. Sew (1) dark blue hexie to one yellow hexie. Using (1) additional dark blue hexie, combine the double yellow units and the yellow/blue unit to form a long chain of hexies. Join this unit to the red (10) hexie chain made in step 16. (See Fig. 22)

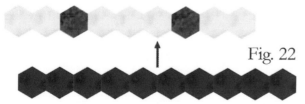

Fig. 22

18. Sew together (1) red and (1) yellow hexie; repeat (3) times. Sew together (2) blue hexies and (1) blue and (1) red hexie.

21. Add an additional red hexie to the red/blue unit. Join this to the end of the red/yellow unit made in the previous step. Hexies should go in order R/Y/R/Y/R/Y/R/B/R.

22. Join blue double hexie made previously to (1) of the red (6) hexie units. Add an additional double red hexie to the end of this unit following the double blue hexie unit. Join these three units together. (See Fig. 23)

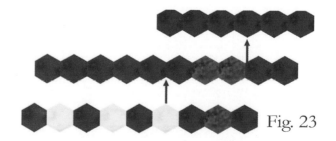

Fig. 23

23. Join sections made in steps 17-23 to bottom and top respectively of previously made fish body. (See Fig. 24)

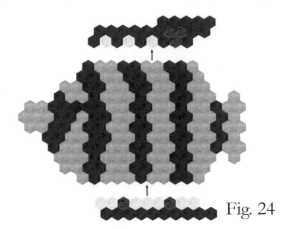

Fig. 24

24. Sew together (2) green hexies to make a double hexie unit; repeat for a total of (33) double units. Add (1) additional green hexie to (7) of these units to make (7) triple hexie chains. Using figures 25-30 as references, join these units together to form the *seaweed*.

25. Apply a thin layer of glue to back of constructed units, and using placement guide on page 49 as a reference, glue to precut blue batik backing fabric. Heat set.

26. Using a narrow *zig-zag* stitch hexies to background fabric.

27. Quilt was quilted using a wavy water-like background filler. Ribbon candy was quilted in the *seaweed* and random wavy lines in fish for *scales*. I repeated the wavy water-like background filler on one of the 17½" X 5" blue batik sections. (This will be the bottom of the bag) (See quilting diagram page 50.)

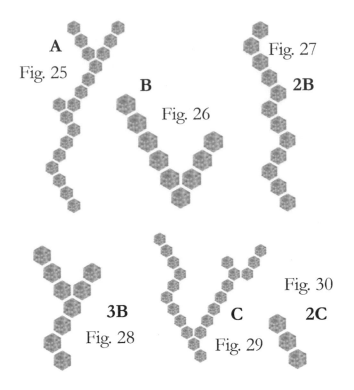

A
Fig. 25
B
Fig. 26
Fig. 27
2B

3B
Fig. 28
C
Fig. 29
Fig. 30
2C

Bag Assembly

1. Trim the quilt to 42" X 17½" and the bottom section to 17½" X 5". Using a circle template (I used a 4" diameter circle) mark corners and trim. (See Fig. 1 & 2)

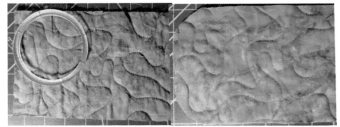

Fig. 1   Fig. 2

2. Bring together the short sides of the *quilt*, right sides together and sew together using a ½" seam allowance. Press open. (See Fig. 3)

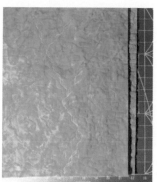

Fig. 3

3. Find the center of one of the long sides of the quilted bottom section and match this to the seam sewn in the previous step. Carefully pin the bottom piece to the *quilt* section gently easing to fit. Sew using a ½" seam allowance (See Fig. 4)

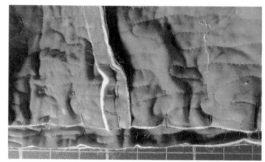

Fig. 4

4. Fold 4" X 32" strip in half, right sides together, to make a 2" X 32" strip. Sew the long raw edges together using a ½" seam allowance. Do not sew short ends closed. Turn right side out; repeat to make second strap.

5. Pin raw edges of strap to right side of bag. Making sure not to twist straps. Repeat with second strap on opposite side of bag. Sew using a ¼" seam. Back stitch to reinforce.

6. Fold over one long edge of the 15½" X 8" section ¼" wrong sides together; press; turn under ¼" again; press. Sew close to turned edge. (This will be the top.)

7. Fold under ¼" wrong sides together; press; on remaining (3) sides. Mark vertical lines on pocket from top to bottom starting on the left side at 2", 4", 6" and 12". (See Fig. 5)

Fig. 5

8. Center on 42" X 17½" lining section lengthwise and 3" from the top. Top-stitch close to the edge of the pocket on sides and bottom.

9. Sew along lines marked in step 34. Sewing from top to bottom of pocket to make partitions.

10. Repeat steps 2 & 3 using the dark blue batik lining sections. Note: When sewing the seam in step 2 leave open a section for turning. (See Fig 6)

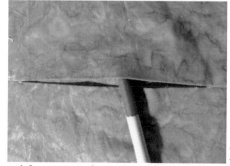

Fig. 6

11. Right sides together, making sure straps are not caught in the seam, pin lining to bag. Sew using a ½" seam. Turn right side out through opening left in lining. Whip stitch opening closed.

Placement Diagram

49

Quilting Diagram

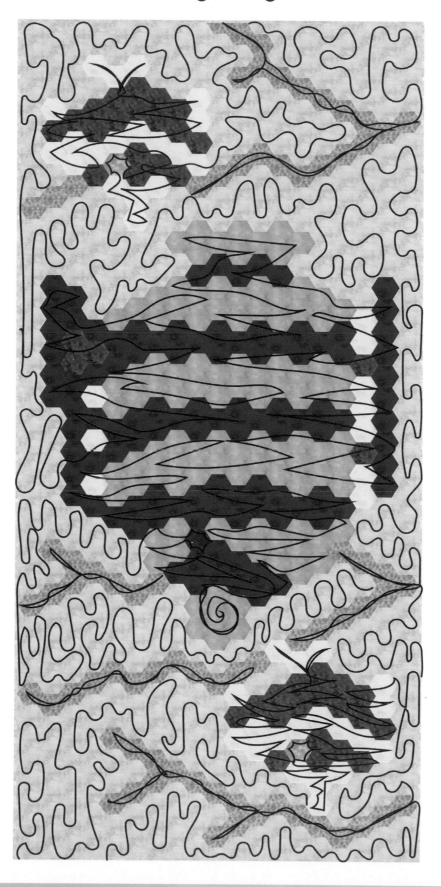

Up, Up, and Away

Finished quilt size 37" X 33"

Let your imagination soar with this bright and quirky wall hanging. Perfectly sized to add color and fun to any room..

Materials

Yardage is based on 42" wide fabric

 Fat quarter orange print

 $\frac{1}{8}$ yd medium green print

 1 yd light blue
includes facing

 $\frac{1}{8}$ yd purple tonal

 $\frac{3}{8}$ yd med/dark blue print

 $\frac{3}{8}$ yd red tonal

 $\frac{1}{8}$ yd brown tonal

1 yd coordinating fabric of your choice for backing.

Hexie Requirements (⅝")

 143 dark red hexagons

 110 dark blue hexagons

 38 brown/orange hexagons

 9 orange hexagons

 30 green hexagons

 24 purple hexagons

Total number of hexagon foundations needed for this project: 354.

Assembling the Quilt

Prepare the required number of each color hexagons, as per the instructions in the *Prepping the Hexies* section. (Page 9)

---✳---

From light blue fabric cut

(1) 33½" X 37½"

(2) 33½" X 2"

(2) 37" X 2"

---✳---

Balloon A

1. Sew together a blue and a red hexie.. Continue around the center hexagons to create the center *standard flower,* as per instructions in Sewing the Hexagons page 14. (See Fig. 1)

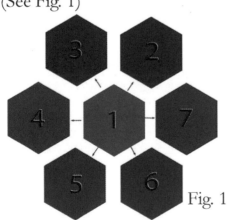

Fig. 1

2. Continue adding hexagons to form additional rings to this base unit alternating red and blue rows referring to Fig. 2.

3. Join together (2) red hexagons. Repeat for a total of (23) double red units.

4. Join (2) of these double hexie units together and add one additional red hexie to the end to make a (5) hexie chain.

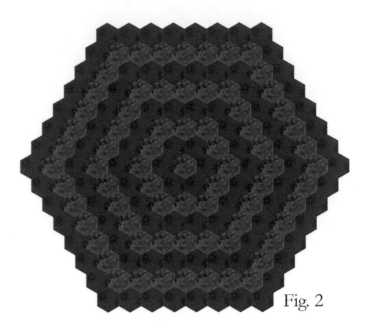

Fig. 2

5. Continue joining double red hexagon units together to make the following units: 1- (8) hexie chain, 4- (6) hexie chain, and 1- (10) hexie chain.

6. Join together (2) blue hexies; repeat for a total of (17) double blue hexie units.

7. Join together (2) double blue units and add a single blue hexie to the end to make a (5) hexie chain; repeat for a total of (3) chains.

8. Join together double blue hexie units to make the following: 1- (4) hexie chain and 2- (8) hexie chain. Join the (4) hexie chain to one of the (5) hexie chains made in the previous step to make 1- (9) hexie chain. Join (1) double hexie unit to another of the (5) hexie chains to make 1- (7) hexie chain.

9. Join units made in the previous steps to the center unit made in step 2 using Fig. 3 on the opposite page as a guide.

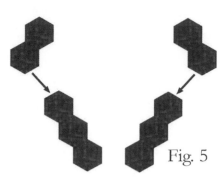

Fig. 5

13. Join (2) triple units together to make 1-
(6) hexie chain. Add (1) double unit to
a triple unit to make 1- (5) hexie chain.
Join (2) double units together to create
1- (4) hexie chain. Join units made in
steps 12 & 13 together to form balloon
basket. (See Fig. 6)

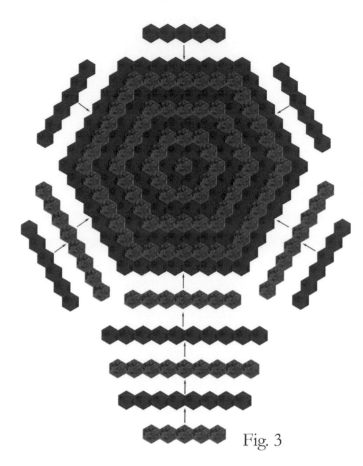

Fig. 3

10. Join together (2) bright orange hexies;
repeat for a total of (2) double units. Add
(1) extra hexie to the end of one of these
double units. Join (1) double orange hexie
unit to the triple chain. (See Fig. 4)

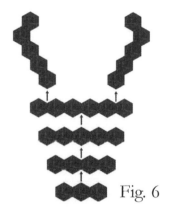

Fig. 6

14. Join *basket* and *flame* to balloon. (See Fig. 7)

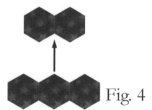

Fig. 4

11. Join together (2) brown hexies to form
a double brown unit; repeat for a total
of (12) units.

12. Add (1) extra brown hexie to (6) of the
double brown hexie units to make 6- (3)
hexie chains. Join (1) double brown unit
to (1) triple unit; repeat. (See Fig. 5)

Fig. 7

54

Balloon B

1. Join together (3) green hexies as per Fig. 1

Fig. 1

2. Sew a row of purple hexagons around the unit made in step 1. (See Fig. 2)

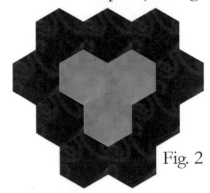

Fig. 2

3. Sew an additional row of green hexies around the unit made in step 2. (See Fig. 3)

Fig. 3

4. Join together (2) brown hexies; repeat to make (2) double brown units. Add (1) additional brown unit to (1) of the double units to make (1) triple unit. Join together (2) bright orange hexies to make a double orange hexic unit.

5. Sew together the unit made in step 3, the double orange and brown units and the triple brown unit made in step 4. (See Fig. 4)

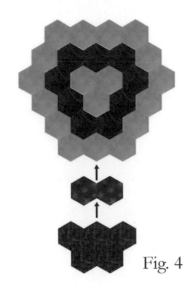

Fig. 4

Balloon C

1. Join together (2) green hexies; repeat to make (5) double green hexie units.

2. Join together (2) purple hexies; repeat to make (7) double purple units.

3. Using Fig. 1-5 as reference join these units with the remaining single purple and green units to form the stripes of the balloon.

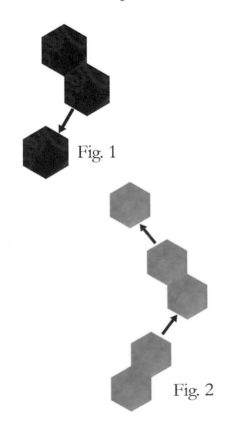

Fig. 1

Fig. 2

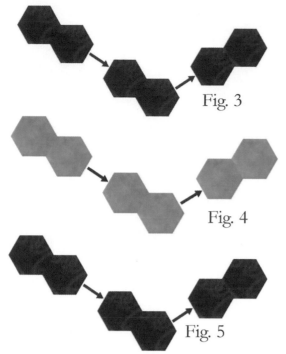

Fig. 3

Fig. 4

Fig. 5

4. Join together (2) brown hexies; repeat to make (2) double brown units. Add (1) additional brown unit to (1) of the double units to make (1) triple unit. Join together (2) bright orange hexies to make a double orange hexie unit.

5. Sew together the unit made in step 3, the double orange and brown units and the triple brown unit made in step 4. (See Fig. 6)

Fig. 6

6. Apply a thin layer of glue to the backs of the balloons and using the placement guide on page 57 as a reference, position them on the 33½" X 37½" blue background fabric.

7. Quilt was quited using a swirling wind-like background filler. Continuous curves were quilted in the baskets, and swirls and loops in the balloons. See the quilting guide on page 58 as a reference.

8. A facing was applied instead of a binding to create the appearance of an uninterrupted sky. (You can find a variety of YouTube videos on how to apply a simple facing, if you are unfamiliar with this technique.)

Placement Diagram

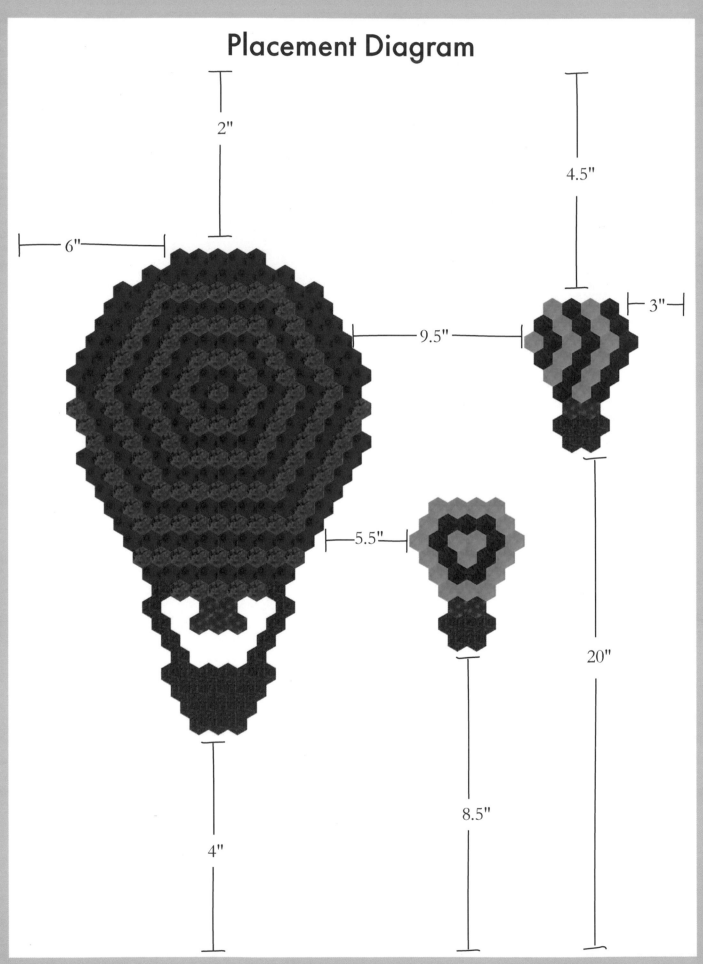

2"

4.5"

6"

3"

9.5"

5.5"

20"

4"

8.5"

Quilting Diagram

Flutterby, Butterfly

Finished quilt size 33½" X 32"

Let your sense of color fly free with this whimsical butterfly quilt.

Materials

Yardage is based on 42" wide fabric

 1 yd medium blue *includes borders and binding*

 1 yd light blue

 ⅜ yd purple batik

 ⅜ yd red tonal/batik

 ⅛ yd bright yellow

 ⅛ yd medium brown

1 yd coordinating fabric of your choice for backing.

Hexie Requirements (⅝")

 122 red tonal hexagons

 160 purple batik hexagons

 92 medium blue hexagons

 42 bright yellow hexagons

 30 medium brown hexagons

Total number of hexagon foundations needed for this project: 446.

Assembling the Quilt

Prepare the required number of each color hexagons, as per the instructions in the *Prepping the Hexies* section. (Page 9)

From light blue fabric cut
(1) 27½" X 29"
From medium blue print cut
(2) 2½" X 27½"
(2) 2½" X 33½"

1. Join together bright yellow hexies to form (2) *standard flower* units, as per instructions in Sewing the Hexagons on page 14. Join together (2) additional yellow hexies to form a double hexie unit; repeat for a total of (10) double yellow units.

2. Join together (2) of the double units to form a (4) hexie chain; repeat to make (4)-(4) hexie chains.

3. Add an additional yellow hexie to the (2) remaining double yellow units to make (2) triple yellow hexie units.

4. Add (2) additional yellow hexies as per Fig. 1 and 2 to each standard flower unit. (Figures show mirror images for Left & Right wings)

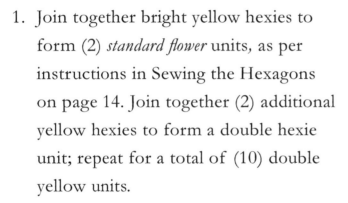

Fig. 1

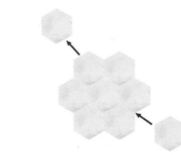

Fig. 2

5. Join one of the (4) hexie chains to the bottom of each of the units made in step 4. (See Figs. 3 and 4)

Fig. 3

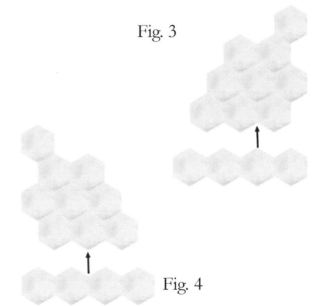

Fig. 4

6. Join together (2) medium blue hexies; repeat to make (2) double blue hexie units. Add an additional blue hexie to each of these units. (See Fig. 5)

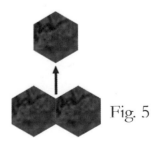

Fig. 5

7. Attach blue hexies to the outside of each
   of the yellow units made in step 5 using
   the same method as you used to make a
   standard flower. (See Figs. 6 & 7)

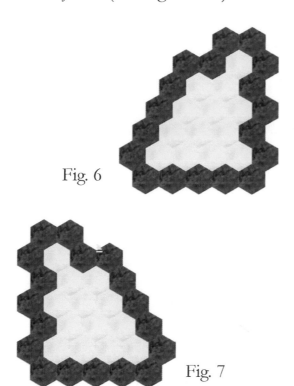

Fig. 6

Fig. 7

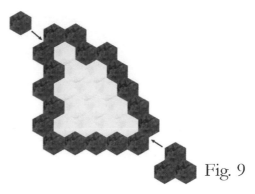

Fig. 9

9. Sew a row of red hexies around each
   of the units made in the previous
   step using the method used to make a
   standard flower unit. Add an additional
   red hexie to the top and bottom of each
   unit. (See Figs. 10 & 11)

8. Join one of the units made in step 6 to
   the unit made in the previous step. Join an
   additional blue hexie to the top of this unit.
   Repeat with the other unit. (See Fig. 8 & 9)

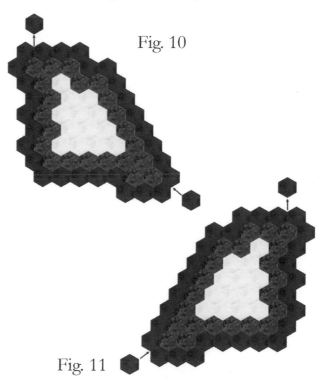

Fig. 10

Fig. 11

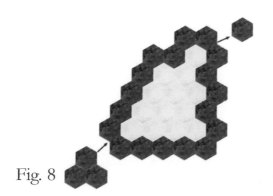

Fig. 8

10. Continuing in the same manner; sew a row
    of purple hexies around the units made in
    step 9. NOTE that this row does not go all
    the way around! Add (1) additional purple
    hexie to the side of this unit; repeat with
    the other *wing*. (See Figs. 12 & 13 on the
    following page)

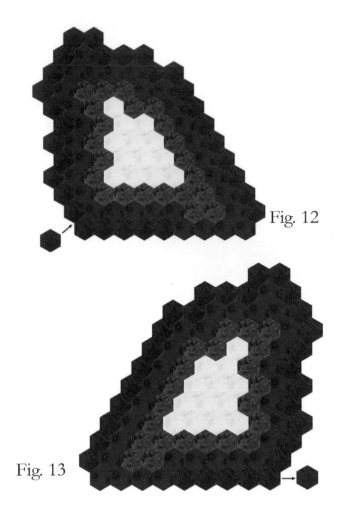

Fig. 12

Fig. 13

11. Join together (1) of the triple yellow hexie chains to (1) of the (4) yellow hexie chains made in steps 2 & 3. Add an additional yellow hexie to this unit. (See Figs. 14 & 15)

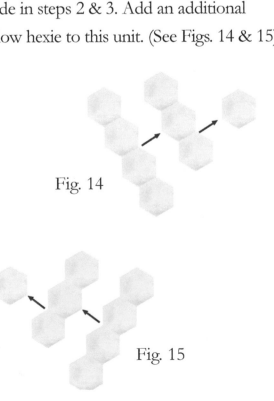

Fig. 14

Fig. 15

12. Sew a row of purple hexies around each of these units adding (2) additional purple hexies as per Figs. 16 & 17.

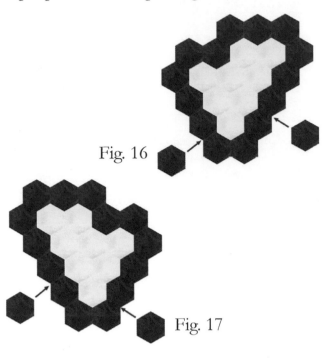

Fig. 16

Fig. 17

13. Next sew a row of blue hexies around the purple hexies added in the previous step. Add (2) additional blue hexies as per Figs. 18 & 19.

Fig. 18

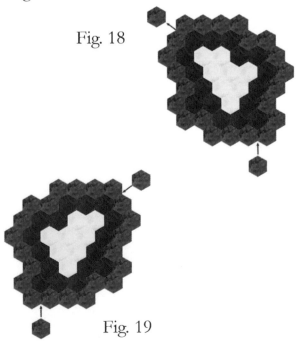

Fig. 19

14. Sew a row of red hexies around the previously added blue hexies adding (1) additional red hexie to each unit. (See Figs. 20 & 21)

Fig. 20

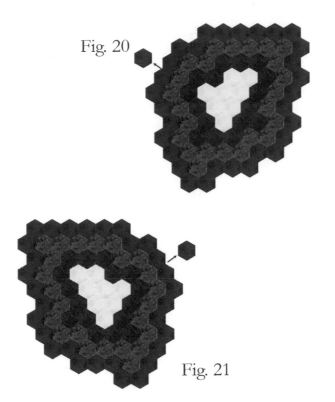

Fig. 21

15. Next add a row of purple hexies to each unit. NOTE that this row will not go all the way around! Add (1) additional purple hexie to each unit. (See Figs. 22 & 23)

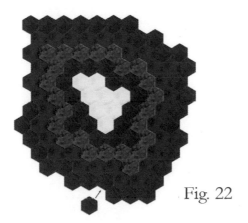

Fig. 22

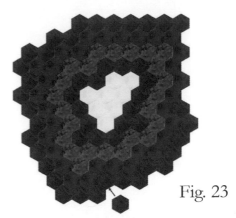

Fig. 23

16. Join together (2) brown hexies; repeat for a total of (11) units. Join (2) of the double brown units together to make a (4) hexie chain. Add (1) additional brown hexie to (5) of these double brown units. (See Fig. 24)

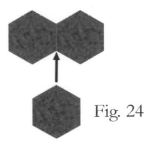

Fig. 24

17. Join together (5) of these units to make a chain. (See Fig. 25)

Fig. 25

64

18. Add an additional hexie to the top of this chain. (See Fig. 26)

Fig. 26

19. Join (1) brown hexie to (1) of the double brown units; repeat to make (2) of these units. (See Fig. 27)

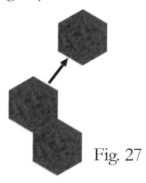

Fig. 27

20. Join the unit made in the previous step to one of (4) hexie chains made in step 16; repeat. (See Figs. 28 &29) (Again these are mirror images for the Left and Right antennae)

Fig. 28

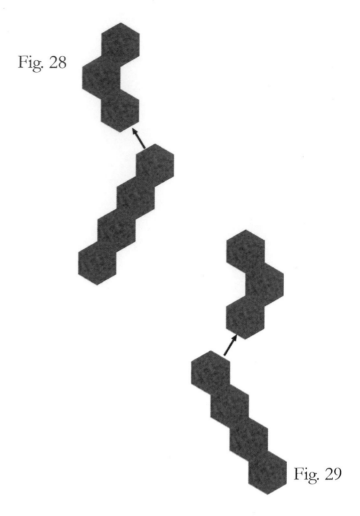

Fig. 29

21. Join the units made in step 20 to the chain made in step 18. (See Fig. 30)

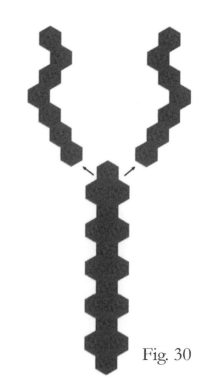

Fig. 30

65

22. Join Left Upper Wing to Left Lower Wing;
    Repeat with Right Upper and Lower Wing.
    (See Fig 31 & 32)

Fig. 33

Fig. 31

Fig. 32

23. Join left and right wing units to center
    body. (See Fig. 33)

24. Apply a thin layer of glue to the back of
    the butterfly, and using the placement
    diagram on page 67 as a guide, center the
    butterfly on the light blue backing fabric.

25. Apply dark blue borders to sides of quilt
    using a $\frac{1}{4}$" seam allowance. Press seam
    towards border. Repeat with top and
    bottom borders.

26. Quilt was quilted with a swirling pattern
    in the borders, and a looping meander
    was used in the background. The butterfly
    was quilted with swirls in the body and
    alternating swirls and loops in the wings.
    (See Quilting Diagram on page 68)

Placement Diagram

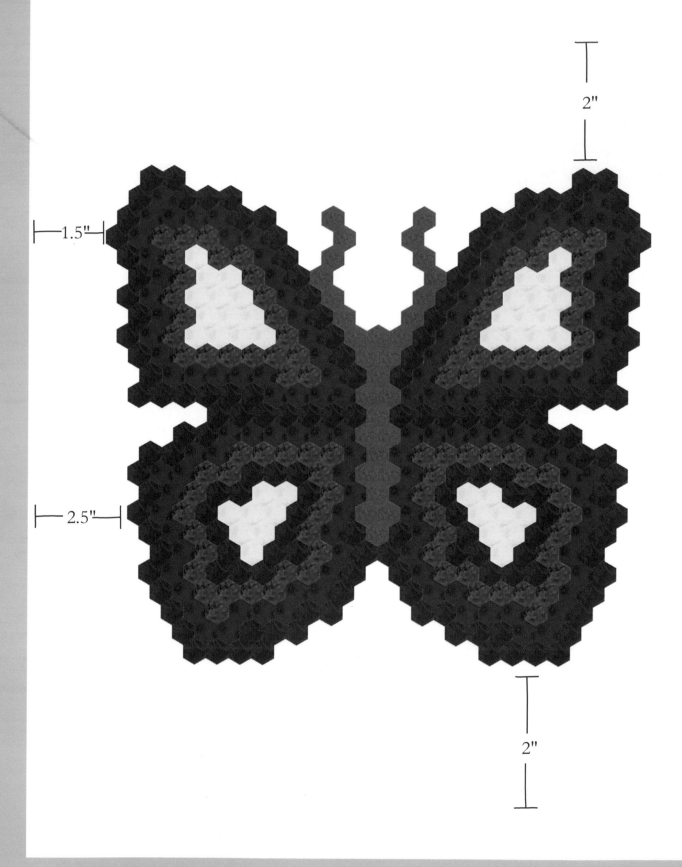

2"

1.5"

2.5"

2"

Quilting Diagram

Bargello De Hexagons

Finished Quilt Size 51" X 35"

Hexie Requirements (1")

 80 dark blue batik hexagons

 36 lavender hexagons

 44 light pink hexagons

 14 medium blue batik hexagons

 68 cream hexagons

 39 medium purple print hexagons

 28 dark purple hexagons

 42 light purple print hexagons

 46 light turquoise hexagons

 52 red print hexagons

 66 beige print hexagons

Total number of hexagon foundations needed for this project: 615.

This lap quilt/wall hanging is a fun new take on a bargello quilt and is sure to brighten up any room

---

Materials

Yardage is based on 42" wide fabric

 ¼ yd red print

 ¼ yd light pink print

 ¼ yd lavender print

 ½ yd medium blue batik

 ⅜ yd beige/tan print

 ¼ yd light turquoise

 ⅜ cream tone on tone

 1½ yds dark blue batik *includes borders and binding*

 ¼ light purple print

 ⅛ yd dark purple print

 ¼ yd medium purple print

Assembling the Quilt

Prepare the required number of each color hexagons, as per the instructions in the *Prepping the Hexies* section. (Page 9)

From dark purple batik cut:

(2)- 2½" X 31½"
(2)- 2½" X 51½"

Center Unit

1. Starting with a medium purple hexie, sew lavender hexies around it to create a *standard flower,* as per instructions in Sewing the Hexagons on page 14 (See Fig. 1)

Fig. 1

2. Join (1) additional lavender hexie to each side of the unit made in step 1. (See Fig. 2)

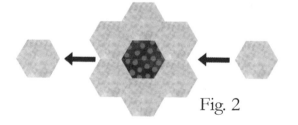

Fig. 2

3. Join together (2) light purple hexies to make a double hexie unit; repeat for a total of (6) units.

4. Join (2) of the light purple double units together to make a (4) hexie unit; repeat for a total of (2) units. Join an additional light purple hexie to the end of (2) of the double units to make two (3) hexie chains..

5. Add a medium purple hexie to the end of each of the (3) light purple hexie chains. (See Fig. 3)

Fig. 3

6. Join the units made in steps 4 & 5 to the unit made in step 2. (See Fig. 4)

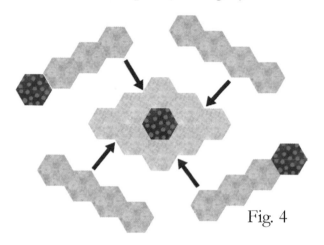

Fig. 4

7. Join together (2) dark purple hexies; repeat for a total of (6) units. Join (2) of the double hexies together to make a (4) hexie chain: repeat to make (2) chains. Add an additional dark purple hexie to (2) of the double units to make two (3) hexie chains.

8. Join together (2) light purple units to make a double hexie unit; repeat for a total of (4) units.

9. Join (1) of the double light purple units to (1) of the (3) dark purple hexie chains and add an additional dark purple hexie to the end of this chain; repeat for a total of (2) units. (See Fig. 5)

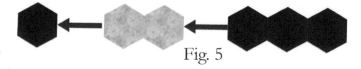

Fig. 5

10. Join (1) of the dark purple (4) hexie chains to (1) of the double light purple units; repeat to make (2) of these (6) hexie chains. (See Fig. 6)

Fig. 6

11. Join the units made in steps 9 & 10 to the unit made in step 6. (See Fig. 7)

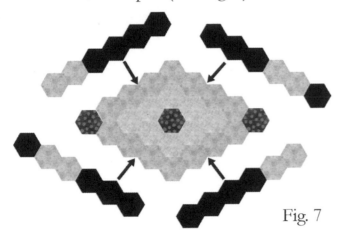

Fig. 7

12. Join together (2) dark purple hexies to make a double hexie unit; repeat for a total of (4) units. Add an additional dark purple hexie to the end of each of these units to make four (3) hexie chains.

13. Join together (2) turquoise hexies to make a double hexie unit; repeat for a total of (8) double units. Join together (2) of these units to make a (4) hexie chain; repeat for a total of (2) chains. Add an additional turquoise hexie to the end of each of the remaining double units to make two (3) hexie chains.

14. Join together (1) double turquoise unit, (1) triple dark purple chain, and (1) triple turquoise chain; repeat to make a total of (2) units. (See Fig. 8)

Fig. 8

15. Join together (1) triple dark purple chain, (1) additional turquoise hexie, and (1) of the quadruple turquoise chains; repeat for a total of (2) units. (See Fig. 9

Fig. 9

16. Join the units made in step 14 & 15 to the unit made in step 11. (See Fig 10)

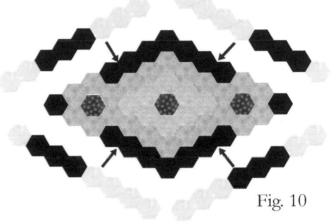

Fig. 10

17. Join together (2) turquoise hexies to make a double hexie unit; repeat for a total of (12) units. Join these together to make four (6) hexie chains.

18. Join together (2) medium blue hexies to make a double hexie unit. Add an additional blue hexie to make a (3) hexie chain; repeat for a total of (4) triple chains.

19. Join together (1) of the turquoise (6) hexie chains, (1) triple blue chain and (1) additional blue hexie; repeat for a total of (2) units. (See Fig. 11 on the following page)

Fig. 11

20. Join together (1) of the turquoise (6) hexie chains, (1) triple blue chain and (1) additional turquoise hexie; repeat for a total of (2) units. (See Fig. 12)

25. Sew together (1) dark blue double hexie unit, (1) medium blue (9) hexie chain and (1) additional medium blue hexie; repeat for a total of (2) units. (See Fig. 15)

Fig. 12

21. Sew the units made in steps 19 & 20 to the unit made in step 16. (See Fig. 13)

Fig. 15

26. Join the units made in steps 24 & 25 to the sides of the unit made in step 21. (See Fig. 16)

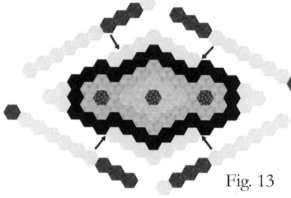

Fig. 13

22. Join together (2) dark blue hexies to make a double unit; repeat for a total of (4) units

23. Join together (2) medium blue hexies to make a double unit; repeat for a total of (16) units. Join these units together to make four chains of (8) hexies each. Add (1) additional medium blue hexie to the end of (2) of these chains to make (2) units of (9) hexies each.

24. Sew (1) dark blue (2) hexie unit, (1) medium blue (2) hexie unit and (1) medium blue (8) hexie chain together; repeat for a total of (2) units. (See Fig. 14)

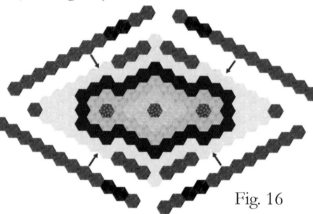

Fig. 16

27. Join together (2) dark blue hexies; repeat for a total of (24) double units. Join (5) of these units together to form a 10 hexie chain; repeat for a total of (4) of these units. Add (1) additional unit to (2) of these units to make two chains (11) hexies long.

28. Add an additional dark blue hexie to (2) of the remaining units to make (2) triple hexie chains.

29. Join (1) dark blue (10) hexie chain, (1) cream hexie, and (1) triple dark blue chain; repeat to make a total of (2) units. (See Fig. 17)

Fig. 17

30. Join together (1) double dark blue unit, (1) cream hexie, and (1) dark blue (11) hexie chain; repeat for a total of (2) units. (See Fig. 18)

Fig. 18

31. Sew the units made in steps 29 & 30 to the unit made in step 26. (See Fig. 19)

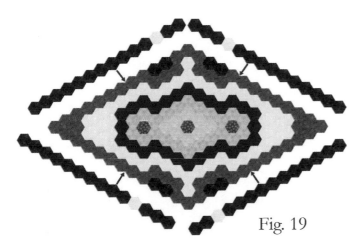

Fig. 19

Right Upper and Left Lower Corner Unit

To make the right upper and left lower corner units sew together (2) of each of the following hexie chains:

(3) dark blue hexies

(5) light purple hexies

(7) lavender hexies

(9) medium purple hexies

(11) pink hexies

(13) red hexies

(15) medium blue

(16) cream hexies

(17) beige hexies

1. Join (1) additional dark blue hexie to the dark blue (3) hexie chain. (See Fig. 1)

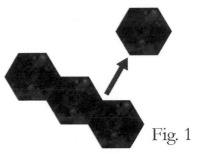

Fig. 1

2. Join this unit to the light purple (5) hexie chain. (See Fig. 2)

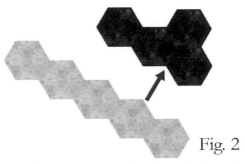

Fig. 2

3. Add the lavender (7) hexie chain. (See Fig. 3)

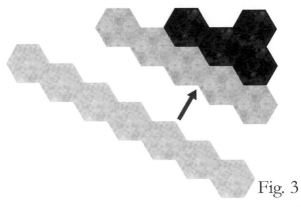

Fig. 3

4. To this unit, add the medium purple (9) hexie chain. (See Fig. 4 on the following page)

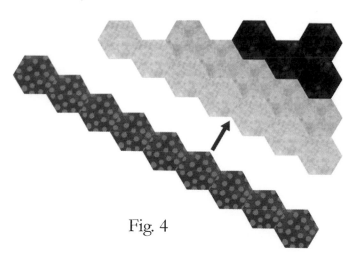

Fig. 4

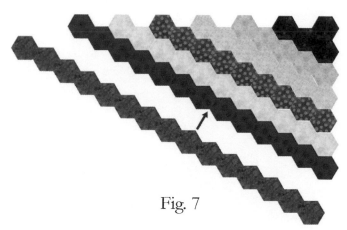

Fig. 7

5. Continue by adding the pink (11) hexie chain. (See Fig. 5)

8. Next add the beige (17) hexie chain. (See Fig. 8)

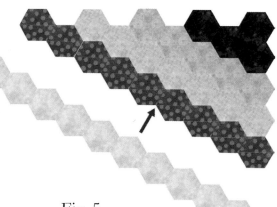

Fig. 5

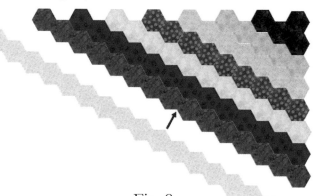

Fig. 8

6. To this unit add the red (13) hexie chain. (See Fig. 6)

9. To finish this unit add the cream (16) hexie chain. (See Fig. 9)

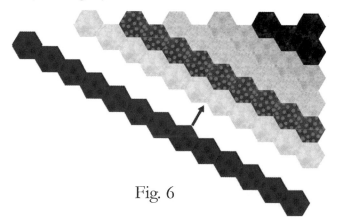

Fig. 6

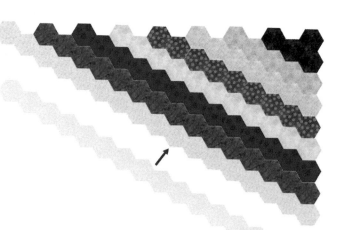

7. To this unit, add the medium blue (15) hexie chain. (See Fig. 7)

Fig. 9

10. Repeat steps 1-9 to make a total of (2) corner units.

Left Upper and Right Lower Corner Unit

To make the right upper and left lower corner units sew together (2) of each of the following hexie chains:

(3) dark blue hexies

(5) light purple hexies

(7) lavender hexies

(9) medium purple hexies

(11) pink hexies

(13) red hexies

(15) medium blue

(16) beige hexies

(16) cream hexies

──────✳──────

1. Join (1) additional dark blue hexie to the dark blue (3) hexie chain. (See Fig. 1)

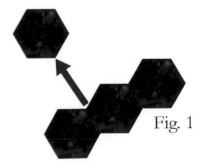

Fig. 1

2. Join this unit to the light purple (5) hexie chain. (See Fig. 2)

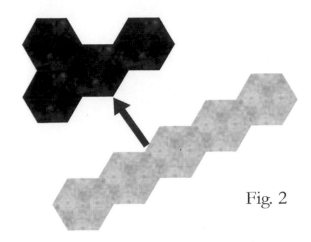

Fig. 2

3. Add the Lavender (7) hexie chain. (See Fig. 3)

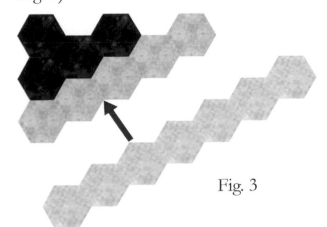

Fig. 3

4. To this unit, add the medium purple (9) hexie chain. (See Fig. 4)

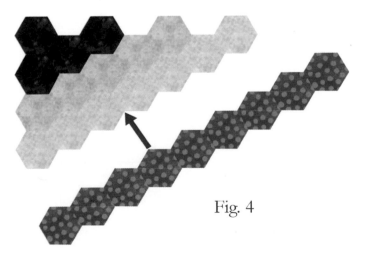

Fig. 4

5. Continue by adding the pink (11) hexie chain. (See Fig. 5 on the following page.)

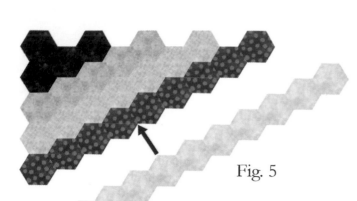

Fig. 5

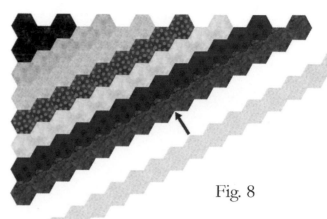

Fig. 8

6. To this unit add the red (13) hexie chain. (See Fig. 6)

9. To finish this unit add the cream (16) hexie chain. (See Fig. 9)

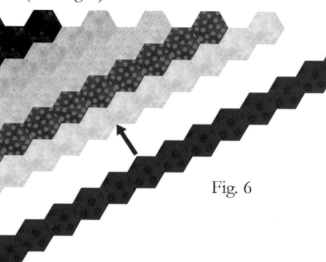

Fig. 6

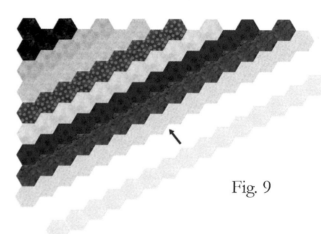

Fig. 9

7. To this unit, add the medium blue (15) hexie chain. (See Fig. 7)

10. Repeat steps 1-9 to make a total of (2) corner units.

Assembling the Quilt

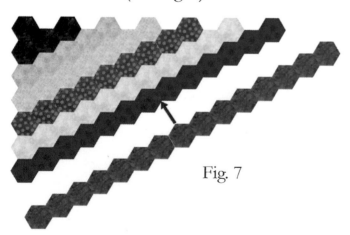

Fig. 7

1. Starting with the Right Upper Corner, and working clockwise, add the corner units to the center unit. See Figure 10 and placement diagram on page 79 for reference.

8. Next add the beige (16) hexie chain. (See Fig. 8)

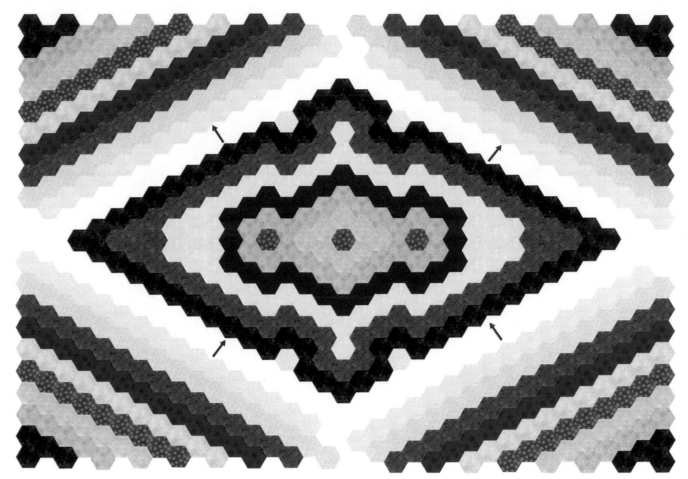

Quilt was quilted using a combination of
continuous curves, loops and swirls. I used a
medium taupe colored thread to blend with
all the different colors. See Quilting Diagram
on page 80 for reference.

Fig. 10

Placement Diagram

Quilting Diagram

Diamonds Are A Girl's Best Friend

Finished Quilt Size 66½" X 82½"

Diamonds are indeed a quilter's best friend in this fun quilt using modern hexies to achieve a traditional vibe.

Materials

Yardage is based on 42" wide fabric

 $3\frac{1}{2}$ yds med/dark purple batik *includes borders and binding*

 $2\frac{1}{2}$ yds medium blue tonal *includes borders*

 1 yd medium green tonal

 $1\frac{3}{8}$ yds light purple

 $1\frac{3}{4}$ yds dark gray

$2\frac{1}{2}$ yds coordinating 108 wide fabric for backing, or $5\frac{1}{2}$ yds of 42" wide. (Seam will run vertically to the quilt top.)

Hexie Requirements (1")

 276 med/dark purple hexagons

 256 medium blue hexagons

 164 medium green hexagons

 302 med/dark gray hexagons

 236 light purple hexagons

Total number of hexagon foundations needed for this project: 1234.

Assembling the Quilt

Prepare the required number of each color hexagons, as per the instructions in the *Prepping the Hexies* section. (Page 9)

From blue fabric cut:

(2) 2" X 57½"

(2) 2" X 77"

From purple fabric cut

(2) 3½" X 61"

(2) 3½" X 83½"

Center Diamond Unit

1. Using the method described in Sewing the Hexies, start with a dark purple hexie and create a *standard flower* unit by surrounding it with green hexies. (See Fig. 1)

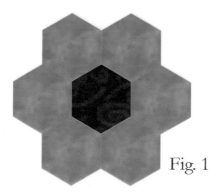

Fig. 1

2. Add a row of light purple hexies to this unit. (See Fig. 2)

Fig. 2

3. Add a third row of dark gray and light purple hexies to unit. (See Fig. 3)

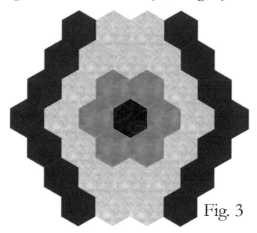

Fig. 3

4. Join together (2) dark gray hexies add an additional dark gray hexie to this double unit; repeat (See Fig. 4)

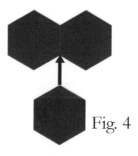

Fig. 4

5. Join one light purple hexie to one dark gray hexie. Add an additional dark gray hexie to the other side of the light purple hexie. Join this triple hexie chain to the unit made in step 4; repeat. (See Fig. 5)

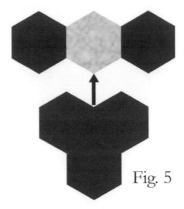

Fig. 5

6. Add the (2) units made in the previous step to the top and bottom of the standard flower unit made in step 2. (See Fig. 6)

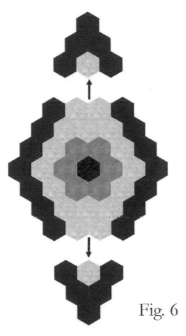

Fig. 6

7. Repeat steps 1-6 to make a total of (6) center diamond units

Blue Diamond Unit

1. Using the method described in Sewing the Hexies, start with a green hexie and create a *standard flower* unit by surrounding it with blue and green hexies. (See Fig. 1)

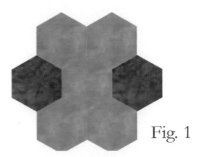

Fig. 1

2. Add a row of purple, green, and blue hexies to this unit. (See Fig. 2)

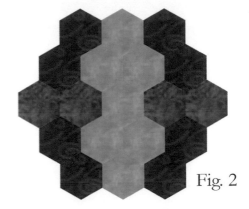

Fig. 2

3. Add a row of purple, and blue hexies to this unit. (See Fig. 3)

Fig. 3

4. Join together (2) blue hexies, add an additional blue hexie to this unit. (See Fig. 4)

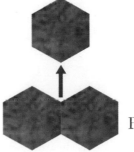

Fig. 4

5. Sew together (1) purple and (1) blue hexie. Add an additional blue hexie to the other side of the purple hexie. Join this chain to the unit made in step 4; repeat. See Fig. 5)

Fig. 5

6. Add the units made in step 5 to the top and the bottom of the standard flower unit completed in step 3; repeat steps 1-6 to make a total of (6) blue diamond units (See Fig. 6)

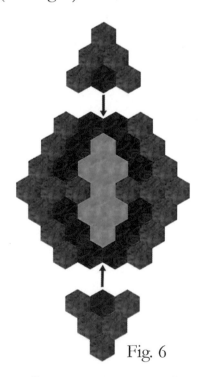
Fig. 6

Purple Diamond Unit

1. Using the method described in Sewing the Hexies, start with a green hexie and create a *standard flower* unit by surrounding it with purple and green hexies. (See Fig. 1)

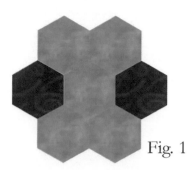
Fig. 1

2. Add a row of purple, green, and blue hexies to this unit. (See Fig. 2)

Fig. 2

3. Add a row of purple, and blue hexies to this unit. (See Fig. 3)

Fig. 3

4. Join together (2) purple hexies, add an additional purple hexie to this unit. (See Fig. 4)

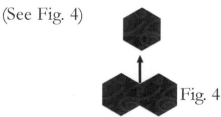
Fig. 4

5. Sew together (1) purple and (1) blue hexie. Add an additional purple hexie to the other side of the blue hexie. Join this chain to the unit made in step 4; repeat. (See Fig. 5)

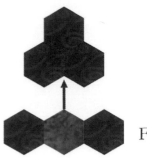

Fig. 5

6. Add the units made in step 5 to the top and the bottom of the standard flower unit completed in step 3; repeat steps 1-6 to make a total of (6) purple diamond units (See Fig. 6)

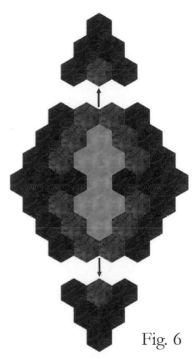

Fig. 6

Top/Bottom Diamonds

1. Join together (1) gray and (1) light purple hexie. Add an additional gray hexie to this unit; repeat for a total of (12) units. (See Fig. 1)

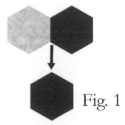

Fig. 1

2. Join together (2) dark gray hexies. Add an additional gray hexie to this unit; repeat for a total of (6) units. (See Fig. 2)

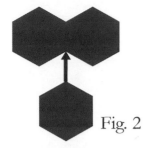

Fig. 2

3. Starting with a light purple hexie add light purple and green hexies to make a standard flower unit. (See Fig. 3)

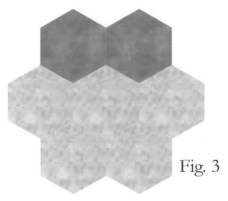

Fig. 3

4. Use green, light purple, dark purple, and gray hexies to make the next row of this unit. (See Fig. 4)

Fig. 4

5. Join the units made in step 1 & 2 to the sides of the unit made in the previous step; repeat Steps 3-5 to make a total of (6) Side Diamond Units.. (See Fig 5 on the following page.)

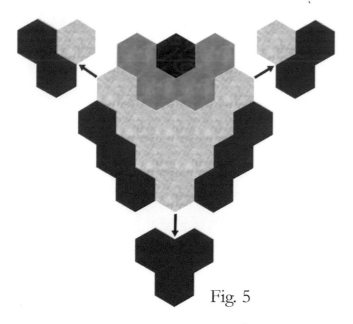

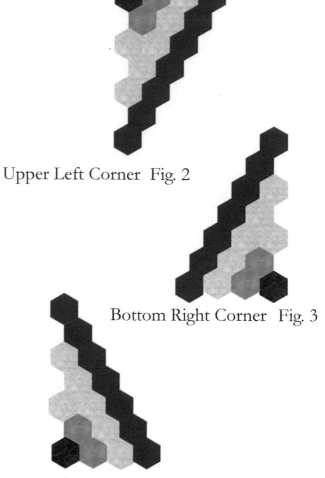

Fig. 5

Corner Diamond Units

1. Join together a chain of (7) gray hexies; repeat for a total of (4) gray units.

2. Join together a chain of (5) light purple hexies; repeat for a total of (4) units

3. Join together (2) green hexies, add an additional light purple hexie to the end of this unit; repeat for a total of (4) units.

4. Join these rows together as per Figs. 1-4. (Note these units are directional and each is specific to its own corner.)

Upper Left Corner Fig. 2

Bottom Right Corner Fig. 3

Bottom Left Corner Fig. 4

Side Diamond Units

1. Starting with a green hexie make a *standard flower* unit using light purple, green and dark purple hexies. (See Fig. 1)

Fig. 1

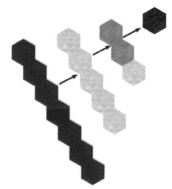

Upper Right Corner Fig. 1

2. Join together (3) dark gray hexies as per Fig. 2.

Fig. 2

3. Join the units made in step 1 and 2 together as per Fig. 3.

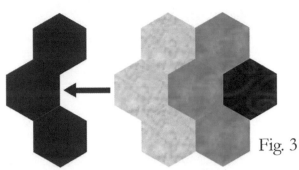

Fig. 3

4. Next join together a chain of (5) gray hexies and a chain of (3) light purple hexies. Using these and (1) additional light purple hexie, join together to form the unit if Fig. 4. Repeat to make (2) of these units.

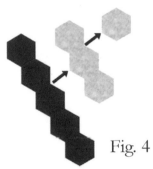

Fig. 4

5. Join together the units made in the previous step with the unit made in step 3. (See Fig. 5)

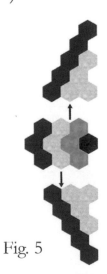

Fig. 5

6. Repeat steps 1-6 to make a total of (6) Side Diamond Units.

Assembling The Quilt

1. Join together (1) top diamond, (1) blue diamond and (1) side diamond unit. (See Fig. 1)

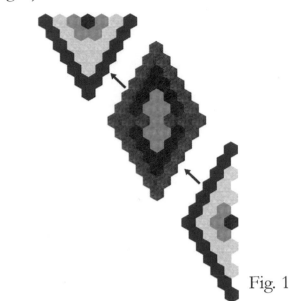

Fig. 1

2. To this section, add Upper Right Corner Unit. (See Fig. 2)

Fig. 2

3. Next join together: (1) top/bottom, (2) purple diamonds, (1) center diamond, and (1) side diamond unit. (See Fig. 3 on the following page.

Fig. 3

4. For the next row, join together: (1) top/bottom diamond unit, (2) center diamond units, (3) blue diamond units, and Right Lower Corner Unit. (See Fig. 4)

Fig. 4

5. To make the next row, join together; (1) top/bottom diamond, (2) center diamond units, (3) purple diamond units, and Left Upper Corner Unit. (See Fig. 5)

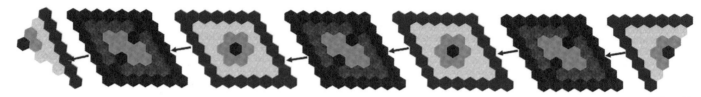

Fig. 5

6. For the next row, join together: (1) top/bottom diamond unit, (2) blue diamonds units, and (1) side diamond unit. (See Fig. 6)

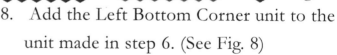

Fig. 6

7. Join together (1) top/bottom diamond. (1) purple diamond unit and (1) side diamond unit. (See Fig 7)

8. Add the Left Bottom Corner unit to the unit made in step 6. (See Fig. 8)

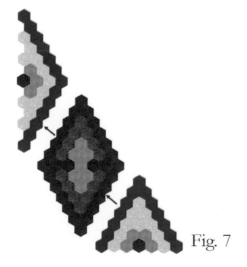

Fig. 7

Fig. 8

9. Join rows made in steps 1-7 together to form the quilt top. (See Fig. 9)

Fig. 9

See placement diagram on page 93, as a reference.
Quilt was quilted using a swirl design in the
outer border and loops in the inner border.
Feathers were quilted in the green hexagon
flowers with a combination of filigree work
and continuous curves quilted in the blue
and purple diamonds. See quilting design
on page 94.

Variation 1

Variation 2

Placement Diagram

Quilting Diagram

Star Brite

Finished Quilt Size 79" X 82"

Hexie Requirements (1")

 112 dark purple hexies

 12 medium purple hexies

 68 light purple hexies

 110 dark blue hexies

 14 medium blue hexies

 73 light blue hexies

 103 dark green hexies

 12 medium green hexies

 72 light green hexies

 94 dark red hexies

 67 medium red hexies

 11 medium pink hexies

 90 dark orange hexies

 58 medium orange hexies

 11 bright yellow hexies

 554 dark brown hexies

 366 cream hexies

Total number of hexagon foundations
needed for this project: 1827.

Materials

Yardage is based on 42" wide fabric

 $\frac{5}{8}$ yd dark purple print

 $\frac{1}{8}$ yd medium purple print

 $2\frac{1}{2}$ yds lt. purple print *includes fabric for borders and binding*

 $\frac{5}{8}$ yd dark blue print

 $\frac{1}{8}$ yd medium blue print

 $\frac{1}{2}$ yd light blue print

 $\frac{5}{8}$ yd dark green print

 $\frac{1}{8}$ yd medium green print

 $\frac{3}{8}$ yd light green print

 $\frac{1}{2}$ yd dark red print

 $\frac{3}{8}$ yd medium red print

 $\frac{1}{8}$ yd medium pink print

 $\frac{1}{2}$ yd dark orange print

 $\frac{3}{8}$ yd medium orange print

 $\frac{1}{8}$ yd bright yellow print

 $2\frac{3}{4}$ yds dark brown

 $1\frac{7}{8}$ yds cream

Assembling the Quilt

Star lite star brite, hexies in the sky with diamonds. This fun traditional hexie quilt will brighten any bedroom, and can easily be modified to fit your color scheme.

———✳———

Prepare the required number of each color hexagons, as per the instructions in the *Prepping the Hexies* section. (Page 9)

———✳———

Additional fabric needed: 2⅓ yds coordinating fabric for backing.

Cut from light purple:

(2) 2" by approximately 86"

(2) 2¼" by approximately 83"

———✳———

Diamond Units

Using the instructions that follow make the following diamond units:

(3) light purple with dark purple centers

(4) dark purple with light purple centers

(3) light green with dark green centers

(4) dark green with light green centers

(3) light orange with dark orange centers

(3) dark orange with light orange centers

(3) light red with dark red centers

(3) dark red with light red centers

(3) light blue with dark blue centers

(3) dark blue with light blue centers

1. Starting with a dark green hexie, add light green and dark green hexies around it to make a *standard flower* unit. (See Fig. 1)

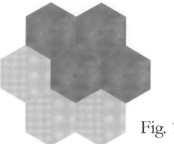

Fig. 1

2. Join together (3) light green hexies as per Fig. 2. Join this unit to the unit made in step 1. (See Fig. 3)

Fig. 2

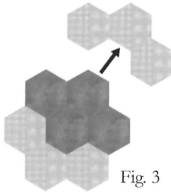

Fig. 3

3. Join together (3) light green hexies as per Fig. 4; repeat to make (2) of these units.

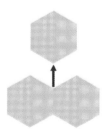

Fig. 4

4. Join the units made in step 3 to both ends of the unit made in step 2. (See Fig. 5 on the opposite page)

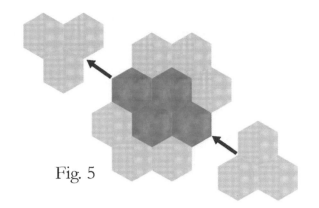

Fig. 5

Fig. 3

5. Repeat steps 1-4 to make the required number of Diamond Units in each of the different colors.

Partial Diamond Units

1. Starting with a dark blue hexie sew light and dark blue hexies around it to make a *standard flower* unit. (See Fig. 1)

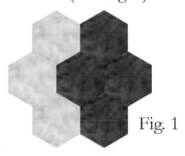

Fig. 1

2. Join together (2) light blue hexies add an additional light blue hexie as per Fig. 2; repeat to make (2) of these units.

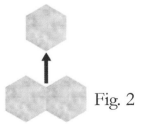

Fig. 2

3. Join the units made in the previous step to the top and bottom of the standard flower unit. (See Fig. 3)

4. Repeat steps 1-3 substituting dark red were it says dark blue and light red where it says light blue.

Star Units

Following these instructions make the following units:

(2) Purple Stars

(2) Green Stars

(1) Orange Star

(1) Red Star

(1) Blue Star

1. Starting with a dark purple hexie, join a row of light purple hexies to it to make a *standard flower* unit. (See Fig. 1)

Fig. 1

2. Join another row to this unit alternating medium and dark purple hexies (See Fig. 2 on the following page.)

Fig. 2

3. To the this unit add a row of alternating beige and dark purple hexies. (See Fig. 3)

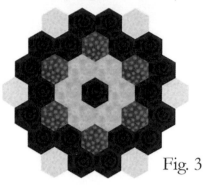

Fig. 3

4. Add a final row to this unit using beige, dark purple, and brown hexies. (See Fig. 4)

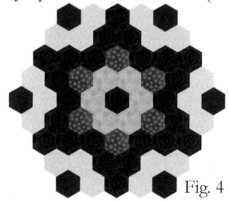

Fig. 4

5. Join together (1) brown and (1) beige hexie; repeat for a total of 18 units

6. Join together (2) of the units made in step 5; repeat for a total of (6) units. (See Fig. 5)

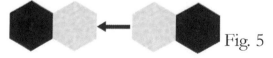

Fig. 5

7. Add an additional brown hexie to the end of a beige/brown hexie unit; repeat for a total of (6) units. (See Fig. 6)

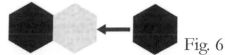

Fig. 6

8. Join together (2) brown hexies; repeat for a total of (6) double brown units.

9. Using one additional brown hexie, join together the units made in steps 6-8; repeat for a total of (6) units. (See Fig. 7)

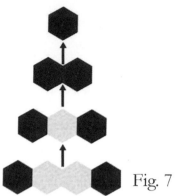

Fig. 7

10. Sew (1) unit to each side of the standard flower unit made previously. (See Fig. 8)

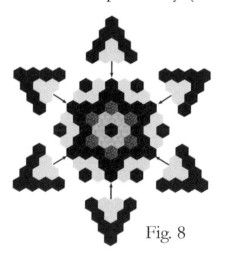

Fig. 8

Partial Star Units

Following these instructions make the following units.

(2) blue partial star units

(1) red partial star unit

(1) orange partial star unit.

1. Starting with a dark orange hexie, sew dark orange, medium orange, bright yellow and beige hexies around it to form a standard flower unit. (See Fig. 1)

Fig. 1

2. Using brown, beige, dark orange and yellow hexies add another row to this unit. (See Fig. 2)

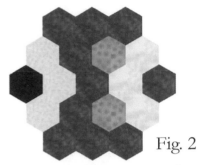

Fig. 2

3. Join together a medium orange hexie and a bright yellow hexie; repeat to make (2) of these double units.

4. As per Fig. 3, join these units to the unit made in step 2.

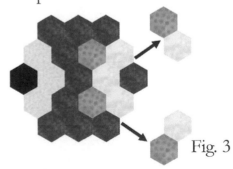

Fig. 3

5. Join together (2) beige hexies; repeat to make (2) units.

6. Join together (2) dark orange units; repeat to make (2) units.

7. Join the units made in steps 5 & 6 together. (See Fig. 4); repeat to make (2) units

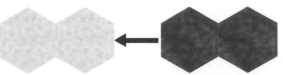

Fig. 4

8. Join together (1) beige and (1) brown hexie add a dark orange hexie to the beige hexie. (See Fig. 5)

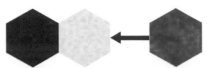

Fig. 5

9. Join the units made in step 7 & 8 together; repeat to make (2) units. (See Fig. 6)

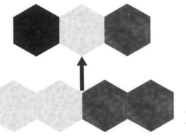

Fig. 6

10. Join the units made in step 9 to the unit made in step 4. (See Fig. 7)

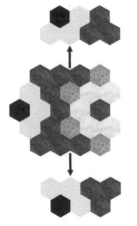

Fig. 7

11. Join together (1) beige and (1) brown hexie; repeat to make a total of (9) units.

12. Combine (2) of these units to make a (4) hexie chain; repeat for a total of (2) units. (See Fig. 8)

Fig. 8

13. Using (1) of the beige/brown units made in step 11, add an additional brown unit to the end; repeat to make (2) units. (See Fig. 9)

Fig. 9

14. Join together (2) brown hexies; repeat for a total of (4) units.

15. Add (1) additional brown unit to the top of the unit made in step 14; repeat for a total of (4) units. (See Fig. 10)

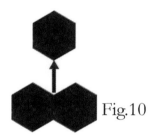

Fig.10

16. Using (1) unit from step 12, 13 & !5, join together as per Fig. 11; repeat for a total of (2) units.

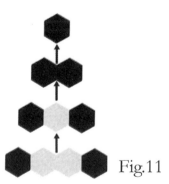

Fig.11

17. Using one of the beige/brown units from step 11, add an additional beige unit to the end; repeat for a total of (2) units. (See Fig. 12)

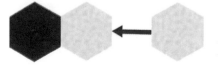

Fig. 12

18. Join the unit made in step 17 to (1) of the remaining beige/brown units; repeat for a total of (2) units. (See Fig. 13)

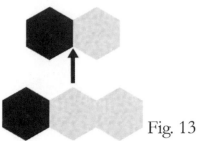

Fig. 13

19. Join this unit to (1) of the units made in step 15; repeat for a total of (2) units (See Fig. 14)

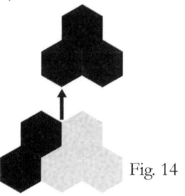

Fig. 14

20. Join the units made in step 16 & 19 to the sides of the unit made in step 10) (See Fig 15)

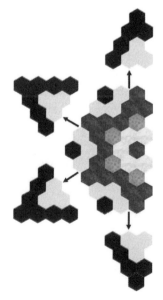

Fig. 15

Top/bottom Partial Diamond Units

Following these instructions make the following units:

(1) Medium red end cap

(1) Dark blue end cap

(1) Dark green end cap

(1) Dark orange end cap

(1) Dark red end cap

(1) Dark purple end cap

1. Join together (2) brown hexies, add an additional brown hexie to the top of this double unit. (See Fig. 1)

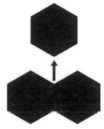

Fig. 1

2. Join together (1) beige and (1) brown hexie; repeat to make a total of (5) brown/beige double units. Join (1) additional brown hexie to (1) of the double units. (See Fig. 2)

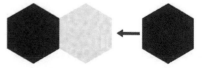

Fig. 2

3. Join the triple Br/B/Br unit made in step 2 to the unit made in step 1. (See Fig. 3)

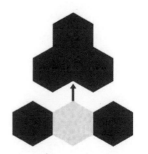

Fig. 3

4. Join together (2) of the double brown/beige units to form a (4) hexie chain (See Fig. 4)

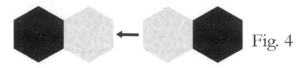

Fig. 4

5. Join this (4) hexie unit to the unit made in step 3. (See Fig. 5)

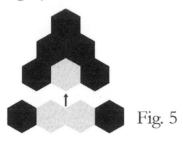

Fig. 5

6. Next join a double beige/brown hexie unit to either side of a dark blue hexie. (See Fig. 6)

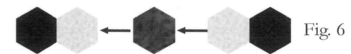

Fig. 6

7. Join the (5) hexie chain made in step 6 to the unit made in step 5. (See Fig. 7)

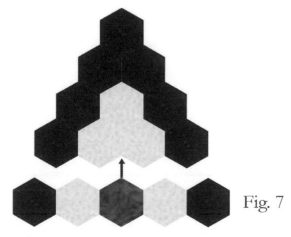

Fig. 7

8. Repeat steps 1-7 substituting the colors listed at the beginning of these instructions for the dark blue hexie.

Top Assembly

1. Join together (4) brown hexies to form a chain; repeat for a total of (12) brown (4) hexie chains. Add an additional brown hexie to the end of (4) of these chains to make (4) brown (5) hexie chains.

2. Sew one of the (5) hexie chains to the top of a light/dark purple diamond and another to the top of a dark green/light green unit. Join the remaining (2) brown (5) hexie chains to the tops of (2) of the dark purple/light purple diamonds. (See Fig. 1)

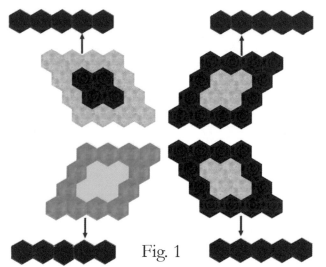

Fig. 1

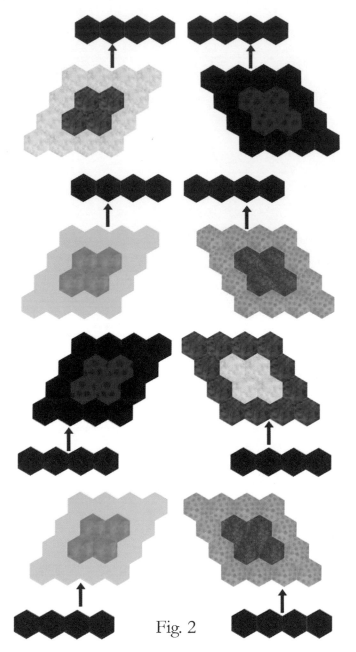

Fig. 2

3. Join the (4) hexie chains to the top of each of the following units: (See Fig. 2)
   (2) light/dark green diamonds
   (2) light/dark orange diamonds
   (2) dark red/light red diamonds
   (1) dark blue/light blue diamond
   (1) light blue/dark blue diamond

4. Sew together dark/light purple and dark/light green with (5) brown hexies units, red, green and purple top/bottom partial units, and light/dark green, light/dark orange, light/dark blue, and dark red/light red with (4) brown hexies units to make the top row. (See Fig. 3)

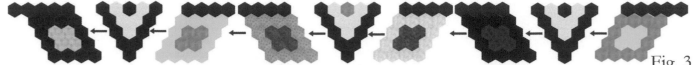

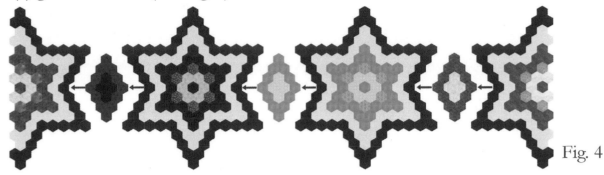

Fig. 3

5. To form the next row, join together (1) partial blue and (1) partial orange star units, (1) dark/light red, (1) dark/light green, and (1) dark/light blue diamonds, with (1) purple star unit and (1) green star unit. (See Fig. 4)

Fig. 4

6. Next, add a brown hexie to the top and bottom of both the red and the blue partial diamond units. (See Fig. 5)

7. Sew the units made in step 6 to (1) orange star, (1) dark/light purple diamonds, (1) blue star, (1) dark/light green diamonds and (1) red star to make the next row. (See Fig. 6)

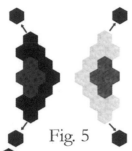

Fig. 5

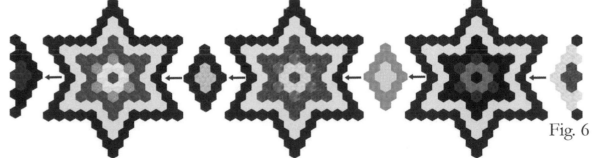

Fig. 6

8. To the row made in step 7, join the remaining regular diamond units. (Not the ones with the brown hexies attached.) (See Fig. 7)

Fig. 7

9. To form the next row, sew together (1) red partial star, (1) blue partial star, (1) light/dark purple diamond, (1) green star, (1) light/dark blue diamond, (1) purple star and (1) dark/light orange diamond. (See Fig. 8)

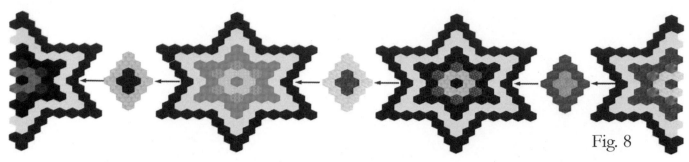

Fig. 8

10. Next, sew together dark/light purple and light/dark purple diamonds with the attached (5) brown hexies, remaining diamonds with the attached (4) brown hexies and the purple, blue, and orange top/bottom partial diamond units. (See Fig. 9)

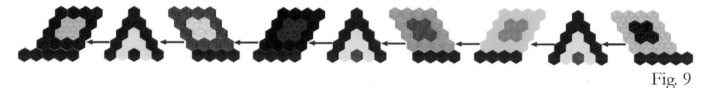

Fig. 9

11. Join the units made in steps 1-10 together to form the quilt top using Fig. 10 on the following page and the placement diagram on page 109 as a reference.

Quilt was quilted with loops in the outer border. Continuous curves, loops, and swirls were quilted in the stars and diamonds, and additional filigree designs were added to the diamond centers.

Fig. 10

Variation 1

Variation 2

Placement Diagram

Hexagon Jubilee

Finished Quilt Size 76" X 85"

A jubilee of hexie flowers that will let you plan a truly colorful garden.

Hexie Requirements (1")

58 dark purple hexies

29 medium purple hexies

53 medium/dark purple hexies

27 light purple hexies

31 dark pink hexies

58 red hexies

32 medium pink hexies

17 light pink hexies

63 dark orange hexies

31 medium orange hexies

27 bright yellow hexies

58 med/dark blue hexies

29 light/med blue hexies

63 dark green hexies

32 light/med green hexies

29 med/dark green hexies

15 light green hexies

641 light/med beige hexies

376 medium brown hexies

Materials

Yardage is based on 42" wide fabric

⅜ yd dark purple print

¼ yd medium purple print

⅜ yd med/dark purple print

¼ yd light purple mottled

⅜ yd red print

¼ yd dark pink print

¼ yd medium pink print

¼ yd light pink print

⅜ dark orange print

¼ yd medium orange print

¼ yd bright yellow mottled

⅜ yd med/dark blue print

¼ yd light/med blue print

⅜ yd dark green print

¼ yd light/med green print

¼ yd med/dark green print

¼ yd light green print

3¾ yds light/med beige

2¼ yds medium brown

Assembling the Quilt

Total number of hexagon foundations needed for this project: 1669.

Additional fabric: 3 yds coordinating 108 wide fabric for backing and facing strips.

After quilting, cut: (4) strips approximately 87" long by 4½" wide from leftover backing fabric

━━━━◆━━━━

Prepare the required number of each color hexagons, as per the instructions in the *Prepping the Hexies* section. (Page 9) If using the facing method, do not prep the following number of hexies until the side and top/bottom full/partial *flower* instructions. (Hexies will need to be cut out using an exact ¼" seam allowance)

(4) dark purple hexies

(5) medium purple hexies

(2) medium/dark purple hexies

(3) light purple hexies

(4) dark red hexies

(6) dark pink hexies

(8) medium pink hexies

(11) light pink hexies

(6) dark orange hexies

(7) medium orange hexies

(4) medium/dark blue hexies

(5) light/medium blue hexies

(6) dark green hexies

(2) medium/dark green hexies

(8) light/medium green hexies

(3) light green hexies

(56) light/medium beige hexies

(22) medium brown hexies

Flower Units

1. Starting with a bright yellow hexie, join light purple hexies around it to form a *standard flower unit* as per the instructions in Sewing the Hexies page 14. (See Fig. 1)

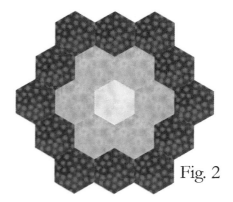

Fig. 1

2. Next add a row of med/dark purple hexies to the unit made in step 1. (See Fig. 2)

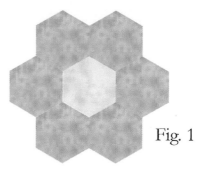

Fig. 2

3. Finish unit by adding a row of light/med beige hexies. (See Fig. 3)

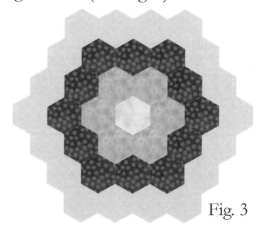

Fig. 3

4. Repeat steps 1-3 to make the following number of standard flower units.

(4) Dark with Medium Purple Units

(4) Medium with Light Purple Units

(4) Dark with Medium Green Units

(2) Medium with Light Green Units

(4) Dark with Medium Orange Units

(4) Dark with Medium Red Units

(1) Medium with Light Pink Unit

(4) Dark with Medium Blue Units

Remaining Units

Before assembling the remaining units, you will need to finish prepping the hexies held in reserve. The hexies will be prepped in one of four ways as per Figs. 1-4. Prep the following hexies for each type.

Type 1 (See Fig. 1)

(4) light/medium green

(2) light green

(2) medium orange

(4) dark pink

(6) light pink

(2) light purple

(2) medium purple

(1) light/medium blue

(20) beige

Type 1

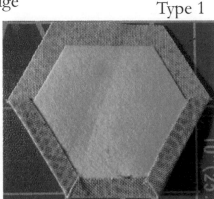

Fig. 1

Type 2 (See Fig. 2)

(1) medium/dark blue

(2) dark blue

(4) dark green

(2) medium/dark green

(1) light green

(6) medium pink

(2) dark pink

(3) light pink

(4) dark red

(2) dark orange

(1) medium orange

(2) dark purple

(2) medium/dark purple

(1) medium purple

(1) light purple

(2) light/medium green

(10) brown

Type 2

Fig. 2

Type 3 (See Fig. 3)

(4) beige

Type 3

Fig. 3

114

Type 4: (See Fig. 4)

(2) dark blue

(2) medium blue

(4) dark orange

(4) medium orange

(2) dark green

(2) light/medium green

(2) dark purple

(2) medium purple

(2) light pink

(2) medium pink

(12) brown

(32) beige

Type 4

Fig. 4

Partial Side Flower Units

For the following instructions, the blue arrow will indicate the sides of the hexies that have not been turned under. (#'s on hexies indicate the type of prep.)

1. Join together (2) Type 1 and (1) Type 2 medium purple hexies. (See Fig. 1)

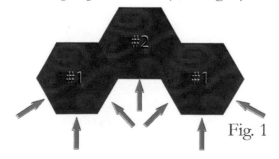

Fig. 1

2. Join (2) Type 2 and (3) of the dark purple hexies that were prepped using the standard hexie prep. (See Fig. 2)

Fig. 2

3. Sew together (7) standard beige hexies and (2) Type 1 beige hexies. (See Fig. 3)

Fig. 3

4. Sew together the units made in step 1-3 as per Fig. 4.

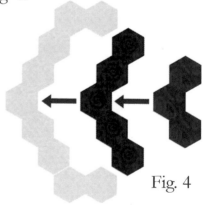

Fig. 4

5. Repeat steps 1-4 to make the following units:

(2) dark green with light/medium green

(1) dark with medium purple

(2) medium pink with light pink

(1) dark red with dark pink

(1) dark orange with medium orange

(1) dark blue with medium blue

Top/Bottom Partial Flower Units

For the following instructions, the blue arrow will indicate the sides of the hexies that have not been turned under.

1. Join together (4) standard prepped beige hexies to make a chain (See Fig. 1)

Fig. 1

2. Join together (3) dark orange and (2) beige hexies to make a (5) hexie chain. (See Fig. 2)

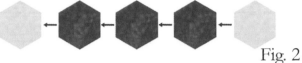

Fig. 2

3. Sew together (2) beige, (2) dark orange, and (2) medium orange Type 4 hexies to form a chain of (6) hexies. (See Fig. 3)

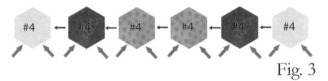

Fig. 3

4. Join the chains made in steps 1-3 together to form the Top/Bottom Unit. (See Fig. 4)

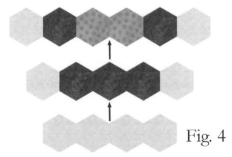

Fig. 4

5. Repeat steps 1-4 to make the following units:

   (1) medium pink with light pink

   (1) dark blue with medium blue

   (1) dark purple with medium purple

   (2) dark orange with medium orange

   (1) dark green with light/medium green

Top/Bottom Flower Units

For the following instructions, the blue arrow will indicate the sides of the hexies that have not been turned under. (#'s on hexies indicate the type of prep.)

1. Starting with a bright yellow hexie, join light purple hexies around it to form a *standard flower unit* as per the instructions in Sewing the Hexies page 14. (See Fig. 1)

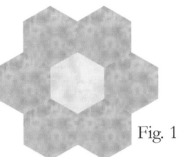

Fig. 1

2. Next add a row of med/dark purple hexies to the unit made in step 1. (See Fig. 2)

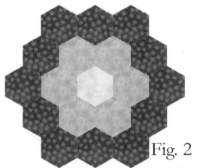

Fig. 2

3. Finish unit by adding a row of light/med beige hexies. Note that (4) of these will be the Type 4 prep. (See Fig. 3)

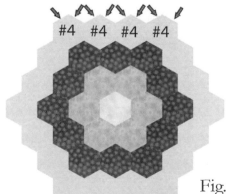

Fig. 3

4. Repeat steps 1-3 to make the following Top/Bottom units;

    (1) additional med/dark purple with light purple center

    (1) dark red with dark pink center

    (1) med/dark green with light green center

Corner Flower Units

For the following instructions, the blue arrow will indicate the sides of the hexies that have not been turned under. (#'s on hexies indicate the type of prep.)

1. Join together (2) Type 1 and (1) Type 2 light green hexies. (See Fig. 1)

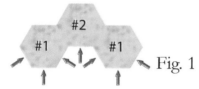

Fig. 1

2. Join (2) Type 2 and (3) of the med/dark green hexies that were prepped using the standard method. (See Fig. 2)

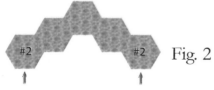

Fig. 2

3. Sew together (7) standard beige hexies and (1) Type 1, (1) Type 3 and (1) Type 4 beige hexies. (See Fig. 3)

Fig. 3

4. Sew together the units made in step 1-3 as per Fig. 4.

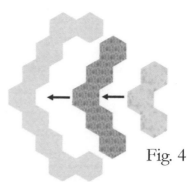

Fig. 4

1. Join together (2) Type 1 and (1) Type 2 dark pink hexies. (See Fig. 1)

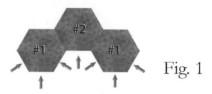

Fig. 1

2. Join (2) Type 2 and (3) of the dark red hexies that were prepped using the standard hexie prep. (See Fig. 2)

Fig. 2

3. Sew together (7) standard beige hexies and (1) Type 1, (1) Type 3 and (1) Type 4 beige hexies. (See Fig. 3)

Fig. 3

4. Sew together the units made in step 1-3 as per Fig. 4.

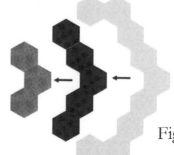

Fig. 4

1. Join together (2) Type 1 and (1) Type 2 light pink hexies. (See Fig. 1)

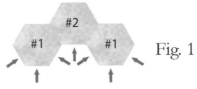

Fig. 1

2. Join (2) Type 2 and (3) of the medium pink hexies that were prepped in the usual way. (See Fig. 2)

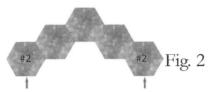

Fig. 2

3. Sew together (7) standard beige hexies and (1) Type 1, (1) Type 3 and (1) Type 4 beige hexies. (See Fig. 3)

Fig. 3

4. Sew together the units made in step 1-3 as per Fig. 4.

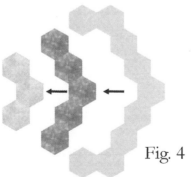

Fig. 4

1. Join together (2) Type 1 and (1) Type 2 light purple hexies. (See Fig. 1)

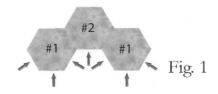

Fig. 1

2. Join (2) Type 2 and (3) of the med/ dark purple that were prepped using the standard hexie prep. (See Fig. 2)

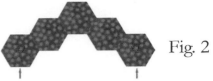

Fig. 2

3. Sew together (7) standard beige hexies and (1) Type 1, (1) Type 3 and (1) Type 4 beige hexies. (See Fig. 3)

Fig. 3

4. Sew together the units made in step 1-3 as per Fig. 4.

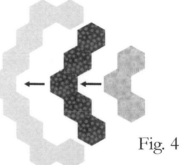

Fig. 4

Assembling the Quilt

1. Join together (3) dark brown hexies to form a chain; repeat for a total of (28) triple brown chains.

2. Join together (4) dark brown hexies to form a chain; repeat for a total of (72) quadruple brown chains.

3. Using the Type 2 brown hexies, join together (2) corner flower units, and (6) of the partial side flower units using Fig. 1 on the following page for reference.

Fig. 1

4. To make row 2, join together (2) top/bottom partial flower units (on either end) and (5) flower units, using the dark brown (3) hexie units to connect them. (See Fig. 2)

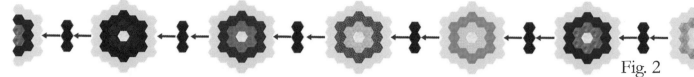

Fig. 2

5. Sew (12) of the dark brown (4) hexie chains to the top of row 2; repeat on the bottom as per Fig. 3.

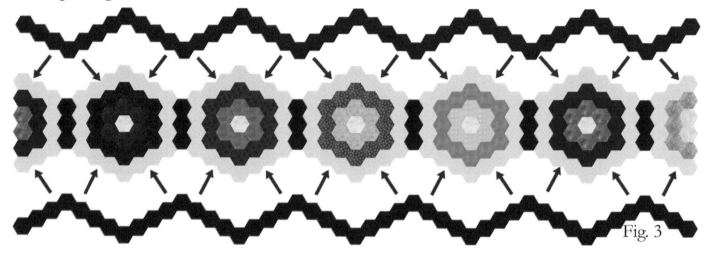

Fig. 3

6. To form row 3, sew together (4) flower units and (2) top/bottom flower units (on either end), using the dark brown (3) hexie units to connect them. Use Fig. 4 as a reference.

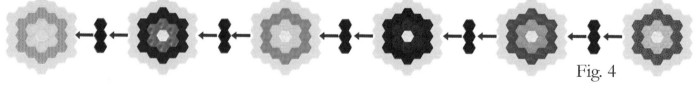

Fig. 4

7. Sew together (5) flower units, and (2) top/bottom partial flower units (on either end) to form row 4, using the dark brown (3) hexie units to connect them (See Fig. 5)

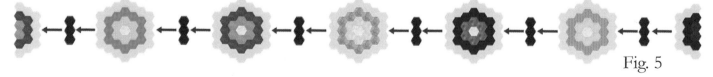

Fig. 5

8. Sew (12) of the dark brown (4) hexie chains to the top of row 4; repeat on the bottom as per Fig. 6.

Fig. 6

9. To make row 5, join together (4) flower units and (2) top/bottom flower units (on either end), using the dark brown (3) hexie units to connect them. Use Fig. 7 as a reference.

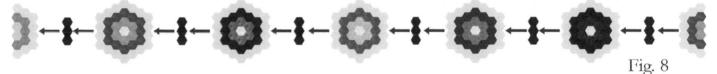

Fig. 7

10. To make row 6, join together (2) top/bottom partial flower units (on either end) and (5) flower units, using the dark brown (3) hexie units to connect them. (See Fig. 8)

Fig. 8

11. Sew (12) of the dark brown (4) hexie chains to the top of row 2; repeat on the bottom as per Fig. 9.

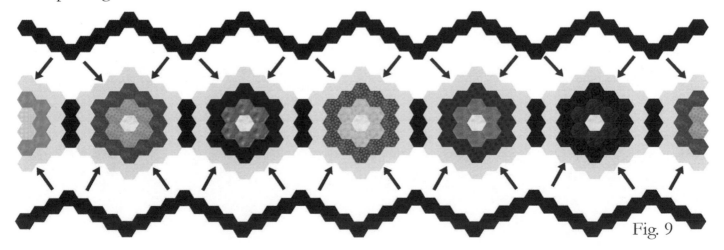

Fig. 9

12. Using the remaining Type 2 brown hexies, join together (2) corner flower units, and (6) of the partial side flower units using Fig. 10 on the following page for reference.

Fig. 10

13. Sew rows 1-7 together. Using Fig. 11 and placement diagram on page 123 for reference.

Fig. 11

Variation

Quilt was quilted using continuous curves
with a simple swirl into the center of each
yellow *flower* center. See quilting diagram on
page 124.

Placement Guideline

Resources

The tools and supplies shown in this book are from the following manufactures and can be found at your local fabric or craft store, Wal-mart, or on the Web.

Quilter On the Run
3500 Daniel Rd
Lincoln, NE, 68506
402-484-7858
www.quilterontherun.com

Superior Threads
87 East 2580 South
St. George, Utah 84790
435-652-1867 or 800-499-1777
www.superiorthreads.com

Nancy's Notions
333 Beichl Ave.
P.O. Box 683
Beaver Dam, WI 53916-0683
800.833.0690
www.nancysnotions.com

Elmer's™ School Glue
4110 Premier Drive
High Point, NC 27265
1-888-435-6377
www.elmers.com

Brother™ Scan and Cut
877-276-8437
www.brother-usa.com

AccuCut™
8843 S. 137th Circle
Omaha, NE 68138
800-288-1670
www.accucut.com

Reynolds Freezer Paper™
http://www.reynoldskitchens.com/freezer-paper/

🌸 About the Author 🌸

Kris Vierra has been a quilter/seamstress for more than 20 years, and a professional longarm quilter for 10 years. She teaches at national shows and guilds across the country, and has won numerous national awards for her machine quilting skills over the years. Most recently, Kris was awarded the Best Longarm Quilting at AQS Paducah 2018, AQS Phoenix 2016, and AQS Des Moines 2016, the PFAFF Master Award for Machine Artistry at the Houston International Quilt Festival in 2015, and Best of Show at the Northwest Quilt Expo in 2014. In addition to teaching, Kris does commission Fiber Art. Her most recent work can be seen on the Album Art for the Australian band the Avalanches' new album "WildFlower." She also runs a full-time longarm quilting business. Kris' classes focus on teaching quilter's how to expand their knowledge base and to break out of their comfort zone. She teaches a variety of quilting classes from appliqué/piecing classes to starting and growing your own longarm business using social media, and everything in between. She believes quilting should be fun and not stressful.

Acknowledgments

I would like to thank my family for their support and patience. My children, who helped out around the house so I could write, and my husband whose encouragement and faith in me helped me to make it through this process. Special thanks go out to my mother. The best editor a daughter could ever ask for.